NEW & NATURAL

Salads
Mary Norwak

BELL & HYMAN

First published 1985 by
Bell & Hyman Limited
Denmark House
37-39 Queen Elizabeth Street
London SE1 2QB

Cover design by Norman Reynolds
Cover photograph by Rob Matheson
Illustrations by Paul Saunders
ISBN 0 7135 2523 1

British Library Cataloguing in Publication Data
Norwak, Mary
  Salads.
  1, Salads
  641.8'3   TX807

Typeset by Typecast Ltd., Maidstone.
Printed and bound by the Pitman Press Ltd., Bath.

CONTENTS

INTRODUCTION

A salad can be much more than a limp lettuce leaf in a sharp dressing, and it need not be considered as a poor substitute for a hot meal. A well-composed salad is a creative dish which blends flavour, colour and texture, and which may be an accompaniment to other foods or a complete meal in its own right.

It used to be assumed that a salad could only be served in the summer months, but there are now so many wonderful ingredients in our gardens and shops that there can be a different salad on every day of the year. It is now recognized that a salad is a much healthier alternative to poorly-cooked mushy vegetables, and many addicts cannot imagine a day on which they do not consume a goodly quantity of raw vegetables and fruit in salad form, which stimulate the digestion and improve the workings of the body.

The art of salad-making lies in a careful selection of ingredients which blend well together. Each ingredient should be prepared separately and salads are best mixed as near serving time as possible so that the ingredients do not become limp and mushy. Cooked vegetables may also be included if they are crisp and well-drained. These are often best if dressed while still warm so that the vegetables absorb the flavours of the dressing.

A dressing may be sweet or sharp or mellow, but the object is to heighten the natural flavour of the vegetables or fruit, not to drown them. A final touch of sea salt, freshly-ground pepper and a sprinkling of chopped fresh herbs will make any salad ambrosial.

Note: All salads serve four people unless otherwise stated.

Acknowledgements

The author and publishers would like to thank the following for the transparencies used in this book.

The Mushroom Growers' Association (facing page 24)
The Rice Information Service (facing page 25)
The Danish Dairy Board (facing page 48)
Del Monte Foods Limited (facing page 49)

A-Z OF SALADS

Artichoke Salad

Artichokes should be very small and young for this dish. Anchovies may be added if liked for extra piquancy.

8 small globe artichokes
1 tblsp lemon juice
salt and pepper
5 tblsp olive oil
3 tblsp wine vinegar
1 tsp chopped fresh chervil or parsley
1 tsp chopped fresh chives
peeled prawns
stuffed olives

1. Wash the artichokes and cut them into quarters. Scoop out the hairy 'chokes'. Rub the cut sides of the artichokes with the lemon juice.

2. Put the artichokes into boiling salted water with a squeeze of lemon juice and cook for 10 minutes. Drain very well.

3. Season the artichokes well with salt and pepper and put into a well-buttered thick pan. Toss over low heat for 5 minutes. Leave until cold, and put into a serving bowl.

4. Mix the oil, vinegar, herbs and prawns and pour over the artichokes. Garnish with olives and/or anchovies.

Winter Artichoke Salad

The winter artichoke has a delicious flavour like the hearts of globe artichokes. This may be enjoyed in a simple winter salad, or peeled prawns may be added to make a complete meal.

1 lb (450 g) Jerusalem artichokes
6 tblsp oil
2 tblsp white wine vinegar
pinch of mustard powder
salt and pepper
1 tblsp chopped fresh parsley

1. Scrub the artichokes and cook them in boiling salted water until just tender but not mushy. Cool slightly and peel.

2. Slice the artichokes thickly and arrange in a serving bowl.

3. Mix the oil, vinegar, mustard, salt and pepper and pour over the artichokes.

4. Leave until cold and sprinkle with parsley.

Asparagus Salad

The salad may be made from canned asparagus, which will not need further cooking. The texture of fresh asparagus is however more attractive.

1 lb (450 g) asparagus
watercress or lettuce leaves
½ red pepper
8 tblsp salad oil
3 tblsp wine vinegar
1 tblsp capers
1 tblsp chopped fresh tarragon
1 tblsp chopped fresh parsley
1 tblsp grated onion
1 hardboiled egg
salt and pepper
pinch of sugar

1. Trim the ends of the asparagus stems. Tie the sticks into 3 bundles. Stand the bundles in a tall saucepan and add hot water to come half way up the stems. Cover and simmer for about 20 minutes until the stems are tender. Drain very well.

2. Arrange a bed of watercress or lettuce leaves on a shallow dish. Remove string from the asparagus, and arrange the stems in a mound on the dish.

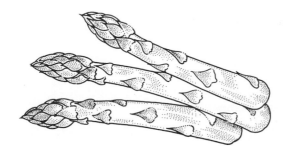

3. Chop the red pepper finely and sprinkle over the asparagus.

4. Mix the oil and vinegar. Add chopped capers, tarragon, parsley, onion and egg. Season well with salt, pepper and sugar.

5. Pour the dressing over the asparagus. Chill for 30 minutes before serving.

Aubergine and Tomato Salad

An unusual summer salad which is particularly good served with fish.

4 medium aubergines
5 large tomatoes
4 tblsp olive oil
2 tblsp lemon juice
salt and pepper
2 tsp chopped fresh chives or basil

1. Wipe the aubergines but do not peel them. Put on a baking sheet and bake at 450° F (230° C), Gas 8 for 20 minutes until the skins burst.

2. Peel off the skins and beat the pulp in the basin until smooth.

3. Skin the tomatoes, remove seeds, and chop the flesh roughly.

4. Arrange tomatoes in a layer on the aubergine pulp.

5. Mix oil, lemon juice, salt and pepper and pour over the salad.

6. Just before serving, toss well and sprinkle with chives or basil.

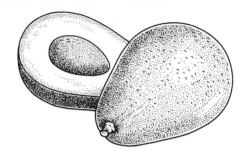

Avocado Salad

This salad should be prepared just before eating so that the avocados do not discolour.

2 avocado pears
2 tblsp lemon juice
1 green pepper
2 large tomatoes
2 oz (50 g) button mushrooms
5 tblsp olive oil
½ tsp mustard powder
½ tsp icing sugar
salt and pepper
lettuce leaves

1. Peel the avocados, remove stones, and cut flesh in slices. Sprinkle well with lemon juice.

2. Remove seeds from the pepper and chop the flesh finely.

3. Skin the tomatoes, remove seeds, and chop the flesh finely.

4. Slice the mushrooms thinly and mix with the remaining vegetables in a salad bowl.

5. Mix the oil, remaining lemon juice, mustard, sugar, salt and pepper. Pour over the salad and toss well.

6. Arrange salad on a bed of lettuce leaves and serve at once.

Broad Bean Salad (1)

Fresh young beans should be used as they will slip easily from their skins when cooked.

1 lb (450 g) shelled broad beans
3 tblsp olive oil
1 tblsp wine vinegar
1 tsp made mustard
1 tsp paprika
1 garlic clove, crushed
salt and pepper
1 tblsp chopped fresh parsley

1. Cover the beans with boiling water and boil until tender.

2. Slip the beans from their outer skins while still hot.

3. Mix together the oil, vinegar, mustard, paprika, garlic, salt and pepper in a serving bowl.

4. Add the warm beans and toss in the dressing.

5. Sprinkle with parsley and serve cold but not chilled.

Broad Bean Salad (2)

This is nicest when the beans are young and small, and the salad is filling so that it can be eaten as a complete meal with wholemeal bread.

1 lb (450 g) shelled broad beans
4 oz (100 g) cooked ham
2 tblsp wine vinegar
1 tblsp olive oil
1 garlic clove
1 tblsp chopped fresh parsley
salt and pepper
lettuce leaves

1. Cook the beans in salted water until tender. If they are large and old, slip the beans from their skins. Put into a bowl.

2. Chop the ham finely and sprinkle on the beans.

3. Mix the vinegar, oil, crushed garlic, parsley, salt and pepper. Pour over the ham and beans and toss lightly.

4. Arrange a bed of lettuce leaves in a serving bowl and spoon the bean mixture into the centre. Serve at once.

Roman Bean Salad

Small young broad beans should be used for this salad, which is particularly good with grilled gammon or steak, or with fish.

1 lb (450 g) shelled broad beans
1 medium onion
3 tblsp olive oil
1 tblsp chopped fresh sage
1 tblsp tomato purée
salt and pepper

1. Cover the beans with boiling water and boil for 5 minutes.

2. Chop the onion very finely and cook in the oil until soft and golden. Add the sage, tomato purée, salt and pepper. Cook for 1 minute.

3. Add a little of the bean cooking liquid and stir over low heat for 3 minutes.

4. Add the onion mixture to the beans and boil for 10 minutes until the liquid has reduced and just covers the beans.

5. Pour into a serving dish and leave until cold.

French Bean Salad

Dwarf French beans are nicest when young and crisp. They should be cooked until just tender before using for salad.

1 lb (450 g) French beans
1 small onion
6 tblsp salad oil
2 tblsp lemon juice
salt and pepper
1 tblsp chopped fresh chives

1. Top and tail the beans. Cut them into chunks and cook in boiling salted water until just tender. Drain well and leave until just cold.

2. Chop the onion finely and mix with the beans. Put into a salad bowl.

3. Shake together the oil, lemon juice, salt and pepper. Pour over the beans and toss well.

4. Sprinkle with chopped chives.

Runner Bean Salad

This may be made with dwarf beans if liked. It is nicest if the potatoes are small and 'waxy' which gives a good contrasting texture.

1 lb (450 g) runner beans
1 lb (450 g) tomatoes
1 lb (450 g) new potatoes
3 oz (75 g) anchovy fillets
1 tblsp capers
3 tblsp olive oil
1 tblsp wine vinegar
2 tblsp chopped fresh chives

1. String the beans and top and tail them. Cut into 2 in (5 cm) lengths and cook in boiling salted water until tender. Drain and cool.

2. Skin the tomatoes. Slice them thinly.

3. Cook the potatoes and slice them thinly.

4. Arrange the beans, tomatoes and potatoes in layers in a serving bowl.

5. Arrange the anchovy fillets in a lattice on top, and sprinkle with capers.

6. Mix the oil and vinegar and pour on top of the salad. Sprinkle with chives and serve at once.

Beetroot Cream Salad

Beetroot should be used when freshly cooked, and this salad makes a nice change from the usual beetroot-in-vinegar.

8 oz (225 g) cooked beetroot
1 medium onion
6 tblsp single cream
1 tblsp made mustard
½ tsp lemon juice
salt and pepper

1. Slice the beetroot very thinly and put into a shallow serving dish.

2. Slice the onion thinly and place the onion rings on top of the beetroot.

3. Mix the cream, mustard, lemon juice, salt and pepper. Pour over the beetroot and serve at once.

American Beetroot Salad

The dressing used in this salad is more attractive than plain vinegar, and brings out the sweetness of the beetroot.

1 lb (450 g) beetroot
3 tblsp wine vinegar
5 tblsp red wine
1 tblsp honey
½ tsp ground cloves
½ tsp ground cinnamon
salt and pepper

1. Boil the beetroot until the skins slip off easily. Cool and slice thinly.

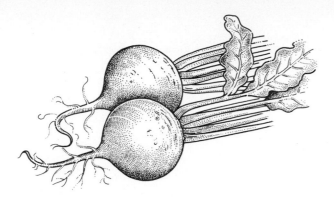

2. Put all the other ingredients into a small thick saucepan. Bring to the boil and pour over the beetroot.

3. Cool and then chill for 1 hour.

Scandinavian Beetroot Salad

The beetroot should be prepared about 8 hours in advance so that it absorbs the flavour of the unusual dressing.

2 large boiled beetroot
1 tsp caraway or dill seeds
6 tblsp boiling water
1½ tblsp vinegar
2 tsp sugar
1 tsp salt

1. Use freshly boiled beetroot and slice them thinly into a bowl.

2. Crush the caraway or dill seeds and pour on the water. Leave until cold and then strain.

3. Mix the strained liquid with vinegar, sugar and salt and pour over the beetroot. Leave to stand for 8 hours.

4. If the flavour is liked, sprinkle on a few extra caraway or dill seeds.

Beetroot in Sour Cream

Beetroot and soured cream seem to be natural companions, and this dish is excellent for a buffet meal.

1 lb (450 g) beetroot
½ pint (300 ml) soured cream
2 tsp lemon juice
2 tsp honey
salt and pepper
1 tblsp chopped fresh chives

1. Boil the beetroot until the skins slip off easily. Cool and cut into neat dice. Place in a serving bowl.

2. Mix the cream, lemon juice, honey, salt, pepper and chives. Leave this sauce to chill for 1 hour.

3. Just before serving, mix the sauce and beetroot.

Red Cabbage Slaw

A colourful salad which makes a change from the usual white cabbage.

12 oz (350 g) red cabbage
Coleslaw Dressing (p. 83)
2 tsp horseradish cream

1. Shred the cabbage very finely and put into a serving bowl.

2. Mix the Coleslaw Dressing with the horseradish cream and pour over the cabbage. Toss lightly.

3. Chill for 1 hour before serving.

Warm Cabbage Salad

Crisp cabbage contrasts with a warm spicy dressing and makes a good accompaniment to grilled meats.

1 lb (450 g) hard white cabbage
1 small onion, grated
4 tblsp soured cream
1 tsp sugar
2 eggs
7 tblsp wine vinegar
1 tsp curry powder
½ tsp salt
¼ tsp pepper
1 oz (25 g) butter

1. Shred the cabbage finely and put into a mixing bowl. Add grated onion, soured cream and sugar and mix lightly.

2. Put eggs, vinegar, curry powder, salt and pepper into a bowl over a saucepan of hot water. Simmer until the sauce thickens. Stir in the butter until it melts.

3. Pour over the cabbage and serve immediately.

Carrot and Lime Salad

If limes are not available, a lemon may be used instead, but the flavour is not so delicious and unusual.

8 oz (225 g) carrots
2 tblsp clear honey
juice of 1 lime
1 tblsp chopped fresh mint

1. Peel the carrots and grate them coarsely into a serving dish.

2. Mix the honey and lime juice and drizzle over the carrots.

3. Sprinkle with mint and serve.

Cooked Carrot Salad

This is a lovely spring salad which may be made with the thinnings from a row of carrots. If they are small, leave them whole, but cut larger carrots into rings or sticks.

1 lb (450 g) new carrots
1 small onion
2 bay leaves
3 tblsp white wine vinegar

1. Scrape the carrots and cook them in boiling salted water until just tender. Drain well and leave until cool. Put into a salad bowl.

2. Chop the onion finely and sprinkle on the carrots.

3. Place the bay leaves on top and pour over the vinegar.

4. Just before serving, toss the salad well. Remove bay leaves before serving.

Marinated Carrots

For the fullest flavour, make this cooked salad a couple of days in advance. It is a colourful and unusual dish for a buffet.

1 lb (450 g) carrots
¼ pint (150 ml) dry white wine
¼ pint (150 ml) water
1 tblsp white wine vinegar
1 garlic clove
1 bay leaf
6 tblsp olive oil
1 tsp made mustard
salt and pepper

1. Peel the carrots and cut into thin rings.

2. Put the wine, water, vinegar, crushed garlic, bay leaf and oil into a pan. Bring to the boil and add the carrots. Boil for 8 minutes.

3. Pour carrots and liquid into a serving bowl and stir in the mustard. Season to taste with salt and pepper.

4. Leave to stand for at least 6 hours, but preferably longer, before serving.

Cauliflower Salad

Cauliflower sprigs may be eaten raw, but many people prefer their texture when they are lightly cooked.

1 lb (450 g) cauliflower florets
3 oz (75 g) anchovy fillets
2 oz (50 g) stuffed green olives
1 small red pepper
1 medium onion
4 tblsp olive oil
2 tblsp wine vinegar
salt and pepper

1. Cook the cauliflower in boiling salted water for 5 minutes. Drain well and put into a serving bowl. Leave until cold.

2. Chop the anchovies and slice the olives and sprinkle on the cauliflower.

3. Remove membranes and seeds from the pepper and slice the flesh thinly. Add to the cauliflower.

4. Chop the onion very finely and put into the bowl.

5. Mix the oil, vinegar, salt and pepper and sprinkle into the bowl. Toss well and chill for 2 hours before serving.

Celeriac Salad

This celery-flavoured root must be lightly cooked before using in a salad. Lemon juice helps to keep the celeriac white.

8 oz (225 g) celeriac
2 tblsp lemon juice
4 tblsp mayonnaise
watercress sprigs

1. Peel the celeriac thickly. Cut the flesh into matchstick-sized strips. Cover with cold water and bring to the boil. Simmer for 2 minutes and drain very well.

2. Put the celeriac into a bowl and pour on the lemon juice. Leave to stand for 1 hour.

3. Add the mayonnaise and toss the celeriac well.

4. Put into a serving dish and garnish with watercress sprigs.

American Celery Salad

The fresh taste and crispness of celery makes an attractive salad which is particularly useful in winter when salad greens are in short supply.

1 head of celery
1 green or red pepper
1 small onion
¼ pint (150 ml) mayonnaise
salt and pepper
lettuce leaves or watercress

1. Wash the celery very well and leave in ice-cold water for 30 minutes. Drain and pat dry with kitchen paper. Cut the celery into 2 in (5 cm) pieces.

2. Remove membranes and seeds from the pepper and chop the flesh coarsely.

3. Chop the onion very finely. Mix the celery, pepper and onion.

4. Season the mayonnaise highly with salt and pepper and mix into the vegetables. Chill for 30 minutes.

5. Arrange a bed of lettuce leaves or watercress on a serving dish. Spoon on the celery salad and sprinkle with parsley.

Greek Celery Salad

This is very good with poultry or lamb, or it may be used as a light first course.

1 head of celery
½ pint (300 ml) chicken stock
juice of 1 lemon
5 tblsp olive oil
3 bay leaves
½oz (15 g) coriander seeds
salt and pepper
1 tblsp chopped fresh parsley

1. Remove celery leaves and trim roots and damaged outer stems. Cut stalks into 2 in (5 cm) lengths. Wash well, drain and put into a pan.

2. Cover celery with boiling salted water and boil for 10 minutes. Drain well.

3. Put celery into a clean pan with the chicken stock, lemon juice, oil, bay leaves, coriander, salt and pepper. Bring to the boil and then simmer until the celery is tender and the liquid has reduced to the thickness of cream.

4. Pour into a serving dish. Leave until cold and sprinkle with parsley.

Chicory Orange Salad

A good winter mixture to serve with beef or duck. It makes a refreshing side dish on the Christmas table.

3 large heads chicory
1 large orange
¼ pint (150 ml) natural yoghurt
1 tblsp cider vinegar
2 tsp light soft brown sugar
1 tsp made mustard
1 tsp lemon juice
salt and pepper

1. Slice the chicory thinly and place in a bowl.

2. Peel the orange and remove segments from membranes. Mix the segments with chicory.

3. Lightly beat together yoghurt, vinegar, sugar, mustard, lemon juice, salt and pepper.

4. Pour dressing into the bowl, toss lightly and serve.

Courgette Salad

Courgette plants can be very productive and it is useful to know of some different ways of serving them, as in this refreshing salad.

8 medium courgettes
1 medium onion
1 garlic clove
6 tblsp oil
2 tblsp white wine vinegar
lettuce leaves
1 tblsp capers
1 tsp chopped fresh parsley
1 tsp chopped fresh marjoram
salt and pepper

1. Wash and dry the courgettes. Do not peel them, but cut across into ½ in (1.25 cm) slices. Put into boiling salted water and then simmer for 10 minutes. Drain very well and place in a bowl.

2. Chop the onion and garlic finely and sprinkle on the courgettes.

3. Mix the oil and vinegar and pour over the courgettes. Cover and leave to stand for 2 hours.

4. Arrange a bed of lettuce leaves on a serving dish. Drain the courgettes, retaining the liquid, and arrange them on the lettuce.

5. Mix the liquid with capers, herbs, salt and pepper. Pour over the courgettes. Chill for 30 minutes before serving.

Courgette and Mushroom Salad

An unusual and colourful salad which may be part of a buffet meal or can be a first course.

8 oz (225 g) courgettes
4 oz (100 g) button mushrooms
4 oz (100 g) smoked salmon or shelled prawns
4 tblsp salad oil
2 tblsp lemon juice
garlic salt
black pepper
lemon wedges or slices

1. Wash the courgettes and trim ends, but do not peel. Slice thinly.

2. Wipe the mushrooms and slice them thinly. Place in a bowl with courgette slices.

3. If using smoked salmon, cut into small pieces. Add salmon or prawns to the vegetables.

4. Just before serving, mix oil, lemon juice and plenty of garlic salt and freshly-ground pepper. Pour over salad and mix lightly. Garnish with lemon wedges or slices.

Scandinavian Cucumber Salad

A simple salad which is particularly delicious with fish.

1 cucumber
2 tblsp wine vinegar
2 tblsp water
1 tblsp caster sugar
salt and pepper
1 tblsp chopped fresh dill

1. Peel the cucumber. Slice the cucumber thinly and place in a serving dish.

2. Mix the vinegar, water, sugar, salt and pepper. Pour over the cucumber and leave to stand in a cold place for 2 hours.

3. Drain off the dressing and discard. Sprinkle with dill.

Cucumber Yoghurt Salad

This is a very refreshing salad, and it is sometimes served as a first course on its own, but is a good accompaniment to spicy foods.

1 cucumber
salt
1 pint (600 ml) natural yoghurt
pepper
1 tblsp chopped fresh mint

1. Peel the cucumber. Cut the flesh into small dice.

2. Put the cucumber in a shallow dish and sprinkle lightly with salt. Cover and leave to stand for 30 minutes. Drain off liquid.

3. Put the cucumber into a bowl. Add the yoghurt. Season with freshly-ground pepper.

4. Add the mint and mix well. Cover and chill for 1 hour before serving.

Dandelion Salad

Dandelion leaves should be young, and a little sugar in the dressing helps to offset a slightly bitter flavour. The plant is rich in minerals, but in excess has a diuretic effect.

1 large bunch dandelion leaves
1 hardboiled egg
2 medium slices white bread
2 rashers streaky bacon
4 tblsp oil
1 tblsp wine vinegar
½ tsp made mustard
pinch of sugar
salt and pepper

1. Wash the dandelion leaves and dry well. Place in a salad bowl.

2. Chop the egg finely and sprinkle on the leaves.

3. Remove crusts from bread. Cut the bread into ½ in (1.25 cm) cubes.

4. Chop the bacon and fry without extra fat until the bacon is crisp. Lift out and drain the bacon and sprinkle in the bowl.

5. Add 2 tablespoons oil to the bacon fat in the pan and fry the bread cubes until golden brown. Drain well and add to salad bowl.

6. Mix remaining oil, vinegar, mustard and sugar, and season with salt and pepper. Just before serving, pour dressing into bowl and toss salad lightly.

Fennel and Lemon Salad

The aniseed flavour of the bulbous Florence fennel is nicely offset by the sharpness of lemons. This makes a good first course, or accompanying salad for fish or poultry.

2 large heads Florence fennel (finocchio)
2 lemons
4 tblsp olive oil
2 tblsp wine vinegar
2 tblsp single cream
salt and pepper
pinch of sugar
1 tblsp chopped fresh parsley

1. Shred the fennel finely with a sharp knife and put into a bowl.

2. Peel 3 strips of rind from a lemon, and cut into very thin shreds. Blanch in boiling water for 1 minute and drain well.

3. Peel 1 lemon and remove all pith and pips. Chop the flesh and mix with the fennel.

4. Mix the oil, vinegar, cream, salt, pepper and sugar and pour over the fennel. Toss well and arrange on a serving dish.

5. Sprinkle with chopped parsley. Slice the other lemon thinly and arrange round the edge of the dish.

Fennel Niçoise

This aniseed-flavoured vegetable makes a good salad. If sprinkled with grated Parmesan cheese, the dish is suitable for a first course, or light meal.

3 large heads Florence fennel (finocchio)
2 medium onions
2 garlic cloves
5 tblsp olive oil
1 lb (450 g) tomatoes
¼ pint (150 ml) dry white wine
pinch of thyme
salt and pepper

1. Trim the fennel and cut each head in quarters. Boil in salted water for 10 minutes and drain very well.

2. Chop the onions and garlic. Heat the oil and cook them until soft and golden.

3. Add the pieces of fennel and stir well over low heat.

4. Skin the tomatoes and remove the seeds. Chop the flesh roughly and add to the onions and fennel.

5. Add the wine, thyme, salt and pepper. Stir well, cover and simmer for 1 hour.

6. Put into a serving dish and chill before serving.

Leek Salad

The mild flavour of leeks makes them suitable for a salad which complements fish or poultry.

8 medium leeks
6 tblsp olive oil
3 tblsp tarragon vinegar
1 garlic clove, crushed
½ tsp made mustard
salt and pepper
fresh tarragon (optional)

1. Cut the roots from the leeks. Trim the tops about 1 in (2.5 cm) above the white part. Wash very well in cold water and cut into ½ in (1.25 cm) rings.

2. Cover with boiling salted water and boil for 7 minutes until tender but unbroken. Drain well and rinse in cold water. Place in a serving bowl.

3. Mix together the oil, vinegar, garlic, mustard, salt and pepper and pour over the leeks.

4. Chill before serving, and garnish with a few leaves of tarragon, if available.

Mushroom and Bacon Salad (page 26)

Leek Salad with Sour Cream Sauce

A good winter salad with a richly flavoured sauce which complements the mild leeks.

1 lb (450 g) leeks
¼ pint (150 ml) soured cream
3 tblsp wine vinegar
1 tsp horseradish cream
1 tsp light soft brown sugar
1 garlic clove
salt and pepper
pinch of paprika

1. Trim the tops and roots from the leeks. Wash the leeks well and cut in thin slices. Cook in boiling salted water for 15 minutes until tender. Drain well and press out surplus moisture. Put into a serving dish.

2. Mix together the soured cream, vinegar, horseradish cream, sugar, crushed garlic, salt and pepper. Pour over the leeks and chill for 1 hour.

3. Just before serving, sprinkle lightly with paprika.

American Wilted Lettuce Salad

A warm salad which makes the best of cabbage lettuce and which is a good accompaniment to meat, poultry or fish.

1 large cabbage lettuce
4 rashers back bacon
3 tblsp cider vinegar
7 tblsp double cream
pinch of mustard powder

1. Wash the lettuce well and pat dry with kitchen paper. Tear into bite-sized pieces (do not cut) and put into a serving bowl.

2. Chop the bacon roughly and put into a thick pan. Heat until the fat runs and cook until the bacon is crisp.

3. Drain off the fat, leaving only 1 tablespoon in the pan.

4. Add the vinegar and cook for 30 seconds, stirring well.

5. Stir in the cream and mustard, heating gently but not boiling.

6. Pour over the lettuce and serve at once.

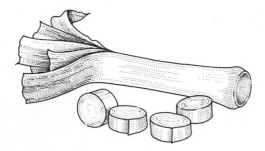

Provençal Rice Salad (page 52)

Mushroom and Bacon Salad

This may be a first course, part of a buffet array of salads, or a delicious accompaniment to fish or poultry.

8 oz (225 g) button mushrooms
2 oz (50g) fresh spinach
6 tblsp mayonnaise
1 tsp dried dill
juice of 1 lemon
salt and pepper
2 rashers streaky bacon

1. Wipe the mushrooms and slice them thinly. Put into a serving bowl.

2. Put spinach in bowl. Cover with boiling water and drain well. Mix with the mushrooms.

3. Mix the mayonnaise with dill, lemon juice, salt and pepper. Pour over the mushrooms and mix well.

4. Grill the bacon until crisp. Crumble into small pieces and sprinkle on the salad.

Greek Mushroom Salad

Try this as a refreshing summer first course, or use as a side salad.

8 oz (225 g) small button mushrooms
5 tblsp dry white wine
5 tblsp water
5 tblsp olive oil
juice of ½ lemon
1 bay leaf
1 tblsp finely chopped onion
pinch of thyme, coriander and fennel
salt and pepper

1. Wipe the mushrooms but do not peel them.

2. Put all the remaining ingredients into a saucepan and simmer for 5 minutes.

3. If mushrooms are very small, leave them whole, but otherwise cut in halves or quarters. Add to the saucepan and simmer for 5 minutes.

4. Leave in liquid to cool, and put into serving bowl.

Okra Salad

Okra is sometimes known as 'ladies fingers', and the little green pods have a slightly gelatinous quality. Okra is now widely available in shops and markets and makes a very good salad.

1 lb (450 g) small okra
8 tblsp oil
4 tblsp wine vinegar
few drops of Tabasco sauce
2 tsp chopped fresh parsley
2 tsp chopped fresh chives
½ tsp chopped fresh tarragon
pinch of salt

1. Cut the okra in half lengthwise. Cook in boiling salted water until just tender. Drain well and put into a serving bowl. Cool and then chill for 1 hour.

2. Mix the oil, vinegar, sauce, herbs and salt. Pour over the okra just before serving.

Greek Onion Salad

A very good first course with wholemeal bread, or the perfect accompaniment to beef or lamb.

1 lb (450 g) small pickling onions
¼ pint (150 ml) red wine
¼ pint (150 ml) water
1 tblsp lemon juice
5 tblsp olive oil
2 tblsp tomato purée
25 g (1 oz) sugar
1 sprig rosemary
salt and pepper
1 tblsp chopped fresh parsley

1. Put the onions into a large pan. Cover with boiling water and simmer for 1 minute. Drain and peel.

2. Put the wine, water, lemon juice, oil, tomato purée sugar, rosemary, salt and pepper into a large pan and bring slowly to the boil, stirring well.

3. Add the onions, cover and simmer for 25 minutes until the onions are tender.

4. Lift out the onions with a perforated spoon and place in a serving dish.

5. Boil the cooking liquid for 5 minutes until thick. Remove the rosemary and pour the liquid over the onions.

6. Sprinkle with parsley. Chill for 30 minutes before serving.

Onion Sambal

A classic accompaniment to curries and other spiced dishes, this also makes a very good salad to serve with grilled meat.

2 medium onions
1 garlic clove
¼ pint (150 ml) natural yoghurt
1 tblsp chopped fresh mint
½ tsp chili powder
½ tsp sugar
salt and pepper

1. Peel the onions. Slice them thinly and put into a serving dish.

2. Crush the garlic and mix with the yoghurt, mint, chili powder, sugar, salt and pepper.

3. Spoon over the onions and mix well. Chill for 30 minutes before serving.

Oriental Onion Salad

A delicious mixture which is particularly good with poultry or ham.

12 oz (350 g) button onions
3 tblsp oil
1 oz (25 g) butter
2 canned pineapple rings
1 red pepper
1 tblsp vinegar
1 tblsp lemon juice
1 oz (25 g) light soft brown sugar
salt and pepper
pinch of ground ginger

1. Peel the onions and cook gently in oil and butter until golden.

2. Chop the pineapple and pepper finely and add to the pan. Cook for 3 minutes, stirring well.

3. Add the vinegar, lemon, sugar, salt, pepper and ginger. Simmer over low heat for at least 10 minutes until the onions are tender.

4. Pour into serving bowl and leave until cold.

Parsnip Salad

The slight sweetness of this vegetable contrasts well with mayonnaise or French dressing. It is sometimes known as 'poor man's lobster salad' because of the texture and flavour.

1 lb (450 g) parsnips
lettuce leaves
¼ pint (150 ml) mayonnaise or French dressing
1 tblsp chopped fresh parsley

1. Peel the parsnips and cut into large chunks. Cook in boiling salted water until tender but not broken. Drain well.

2. Cut the cooked parsnips into matchstick-sized pieces. Place in a bowl, cover and chill for 1 hour.

3. Shred the lettuce leaves and arrange in a serving bowl. Spoon in the parsnips.

4. Spoon over the mayonnaise or French dressing. Sprinkle with parsley.

Summer Pea Salad

Fresh or frozen peas may be used for this delicious salad, which is particularly good served with ham or fish.

12 oz (350 g) shelled fresh or frozen peas
6 tblsp salad oil
4 tblsp wine vinegar
1 tsp chopped fresh mint
pinch of mustard powder
1 Webb's or Iceberg lettuce
2 hardboiled eggs

1. Cook the peas in boiling salted water, allowing 15 minutes for fresh peas, and 5 minutes for frozen peas. Drain well and put in bowl.

2. Mix the oil, vinegar, mint and mustard powder. Pour at once over warm peas. Leave until just cold.

3. Cut lettuce into 8 wedges and arrange on serving dish. Place the peas and dressing in the middle.

4. Chop the eggs finely and sprinkle on top of the peas.

Pepper Salads

Filled cold peppers look very attractive and make a substantial meal-in-one salad. Tuna, cooked white fish or smoked haddock may be used instead of the prawns.

2 green peppers
8 oz (225 g) shelled peas
4 medium potatoes
2 spring onions
8 oz (225 g) peeled prawns
6 tblsp mayonnaise
1 tblsp chopped fresh mint
paprika

1. Wash the peppers. Cut them in half lengthwise from tip to stalk. Remove membranes and seeds. Place pepper halves on a serving dish.

2. Cook the peas in boiling salted water until tender, and drain well.

3. Cook the potatoes, cool and dice.

4. Slice the onions thinly and mix with the peas, potatoes and prawns. Add the mayonnaise, toss lightly and fill the pepper halves.

5. Garnish with mint and sprinkle with pepper. Chill for 30 minutes before serving.

Turkish Pepper Salad

A mixture of refreshing flavours and textures which makes this salad particularly suitable to serve with grilled meat or fish.

2 green peppers
4 spring onions
1 oz (25 g) pine nuts
1 oz (25 g) seedless raisins
6 tblsp olive oil
2 tblsp lemon juice
salt and pepper
pinch of paprika

1. Cut the peppers into quarters lengthwise. Remove membranes and seeds. Slice the flesh thinly and place in a serving bowl.

2. Chop the onions finely. Add the onions and pine nuts to the peppers.

3. Cover the raisins with boiling water and leave to stand for 15 minutes. Drain well and mix with the peppers.

4. Mix the oil, lemon juice, salt, pepper and paprika. Pour into the bowl and toss well. Serve at once.

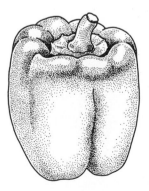

Potato Salad

A firm waxy potato has the best texture for traditional potato salad, and a little onion offsets the blandness of potato and mayonnaise.

1 lb (450 g) potatoes
8 fl oz (250 ml) mayonnaise
1 small onion
1 tblsp chopped fresh chives

1. Do not peel the potatoes but cook them in boiling salted water until just tender but unbroken. Drain well and cover the pan with a clean tea towel. Leave to stand for 10 minutes so that the potatoes cool and the steam is absorbed by the tea towel.

2. Peel the potatoes and cut them into neat dice. Put into a bowl and pour on half the mayonnaise. Mix well and leave until cold.

3. Chop the onion finely and sprinkle on the potatoes. Add the remaining mayonnaise and mix well.

4. Sprinkle with chopped chives before serving.

Hot Potato Salad

A piquant salad which is delicious with cold meat, poultry or fish.

1 lb (450 g) new potatoes
1 oz (25 g) butter or bacon fat
1 tsp plain flour
pinch of salt
4 tblsp wine vinegar
1 tsp sugar
4 spring onions
4 lean bacon rashers
1 tblsp chopped fresh parsley

1. Scrub the potatoes and cook them in boiling salted water until just tender. Drain and reserve the cooking liquid.

2. Melt the fat and work in the flour and salt. Cook over low heat for 1 minute, stirring well.

3. Add the vinegar and sugar and ½ pint (300 ml) cooking liquid. Simmer for 2 minutes.

4. Add the potatoes and finely chopped bacon and stir well. Cover and cook over very low heat for 10 minutes, shaking the pan occasionally.

5. Serve hot, sprinkled with parsley.

Italian Potato Salad

This version of potato salad is lighter than the usual type, and more appetizing in hot weather.

6 medium potatoes
10 spring onions
8 tblsp olive oil
4 tblsp red wine
2 tsp red wine vinegar
salt and pepper
12 anchovy fillets
1 tblsp chopped fresh chervil or parsley

1. Boil the potatoes in their skins. Leave them to cool and then peel. Cut into thick slices and place in a serving bowl.

2. Chop the onions finely and sprinkle on the potatoes.

3. Mix the oil, wine, vinegar, salt, pepper and chopped anchovies. Pour over the potatoes and mix well.

4. Leave to stand for 30 minutes before serving. Sprinkle with chopped chervil or parsley.

New Potato Salad

When potatoes are new and small, they are delicious in an oil-and-vinegar dressing instead of the traditional mayonnaise.

1 lb (450 g) small new potatoes
1 tblsp chopped fresh chives
1 tblsp chopped fresh parsley
1 tblsp salad oil
2 tblsp wine vinegar
salt and pepper

1. Cook the potatoes in their skins in boiling salted water until just tender. Peel them and place in a salad bowl.

2. Sprinkle the potatoes with chives and parsley.

3. Mix the oil, vinegar, salt and pepper and pour over the potatoes while they are lukewarm. Toss quickly and serve at once.

Spanish Potato Salad

A refreshing change from the rather rich potato salad dressed in mayonnaise, which is very good made with the first new potatoes.

1 lb (450 g) new potatoes
4 tblsp olive oil
1 tblsp wine vinegar
2 garlic cloves, crushed
1 small red pepper
1 tblsp chopped fresh chives

1. Scrape the potatoes. Cook until tender but not broken. Drain well.

2. Mix the oil and vinegar. Toss in the potatoes while still hot.

3. Stir in the garlic. Sprinkle with finely chopped red pepper and chives.

4. Serve freshly made and still warm.

Radish Salad

Radishes are often served without any dressing, but in this recipe they are used to make a crisp refreshing salad.

8 oz (225 g) medium-sized radishes
2 tsp salt
1 oz (25 g) light soft brown sugar
3 tblsp oil
1 tblsp wine vinegar

1. Wash the radishes and dry them well. Slice them thickly and place on a shallow dish.
2. Sprinkle with salt and leave to stand for 30 minutes. Drain off the liquid and put the radishes into a serving dish.
3. Mix the sugar, oil and vinegar and pour over the radishes just before serving.

Spinach and Bacon Salad

Spinach is an unusual salad ingredient but it combines particularly well with bacon and a rather sharp dressing.

1 lb (450 g) fresh young spinach
4 rashers back bacon
4 oz (100 g) button mushrooms
1 hardboiled egg
12 tblsp olive oil
3 tblsp tarragon vinegar
salt and pepper
2 tsp chopped fresh tarragon

1. Wash the spinach very thoroughly, drain and pat dry with kitchen paper. Remove stems and discoloured leaves.
2. Grill the bacon until crisp. Crumble the bacon and mix with the spinach in a salad bowl.
3. Wipe the mushrooms and slice them thinly. Add to the bowl with the finely chopped egg.
4. Mix the oil, vinegar, salt and pepper and tarragon.
5. Just before serving, pour the dressing into the bowl and toss the salad well.

Spinach and Walnut Salad

The contrast in texture between the soft spinach leaves and the crunchy walnuts makes this an attractive and unusual salad.

1 lb (450 g) spinach
1 tsp salt
6 spring onions
2 tblsp olive oil
2 tblsp lemon juice
2 oz (50 g) walnut kernels

1. Wash the spinach very well. Remove the stems. Shake the leaves to remove surplus water and then pat dry with kitchen paper.
2. Tear the leaves in large pieces and arrange on a shallow dish. Sprinkle with salt, stir in thoroughly and leave to stand for 15 minutes. Drain and squeeze dry.
3. Place spinach in a bowl. Chop the spring onions finely and sprinkle in the bowl. Mix the oil and lemon juice and pour into the bowl.
4. Toss the salad lightly and sprinkle with chopped walnuts.

Tomato and Avocado Salad

A colourful and delicious mixture to serve as a side salad, or to accompany a mild cheese like Mozzarella.

1 lb (450 g) tomatoes
1 avocado pear
1 tblsp lemon juice
6 tblsp olive oil
3 tblsp wine or cider vinegar
1 tsp sugar
1 tsp made mustard
salt and pepper
6 spring onions

1. Skin the tomatoes and cut them across in slices. Arrange round the edge of a flat serving dish.

2. Peel the avocado, cut in half and remove the stone. Slice the flesh and arrange in the centre of the tomatoes. Sprinkle with lemon juice. Chill while preparing the dressing.

3. Mix the oil, vinegar, sugar, mustard, salt and pepper.

4. Pour the dressing over the salad just before serving. Sprinkle with finely-chopped onion.

Tomato and Egg Salad

In France, large tomatoes are sliced nearly through and then fanned out with slices of hardboiled egg inserted, and served as a first course with oil-and-vinegar dressing or mayonnaise. This is a simpler version.

1 lb (450 g) tomatoes
6 hardboiled eggs
3 tblsp finely chopped shallots or chives
salt and pepper
pinch of sugar
4 tblsp olive oil
2 tblsp wine vinegar

1. Skin the tomatoes and cut them in thin slices.

2. Slice the eggs thinly.

3. Arrange a layer of tomatoes in a serving bowl. Sprinkle with salt, pepper and a little sugar.

4. Cover with egg slices, chopped shallots or chives, and season with salt and pepper.

5. Continue in layers, seasoning each time.

6. Mix the oil and vinegar. Pour over the salad and serve at once.

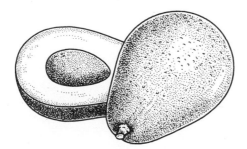

Tomato and Onion Salad

Crisp onions provide a contrast in texture and flavour to firm tomatoes. This is almost a complete meal, served with plenty of wholemeal bread.

1 lb (450 g) tomatoes
2 medium onions
4 tblsp salad oil
2 tblsp wine vinegar
salt and pepper
pinch of sugar
2 tblsp chopped fresh chives

1. Skin the tomatoes and cut them across in slices.

2. Peel the onions and slice them very thinly. Put the onion slices in ice-cold water for 10 minutes to make them very crisp. Drain well.

3. Arrange the tomatoes and onions in serving dish in layers, beginning and ending with tomatoes.

4. Mix the oil, vinegar, salt, pepper and sugar. Pour over the salad and leave in a cold place for 30 minutes.

5. Sprinkle with chives just before serving.

Turnip Salad

This is best made with young turnips and is even enjoyed by those who do not like the cooked vegetable.

1 lb (450 g) small young turnips
1 small onion
6 tblsp olive oil
2 tblsp white wine vinegar
salt and pepper
1 tblsp chopped fresh parsley
1 tsp chopped mixed fresh herbs

1. Peel the turnips and slice them very thinly. Arrange on a serving dish.

2. Chop the onion very finely and sprinkle on the turnips.

3. Mix the oil, vinegar, salt and pepper. Pour over the turnips.

4. Sprinkle with parsley and mixed herbs. Chill for 30 minutes before serving.

Chinese Turnip Salad

The strongly flavoured dressing makes an attractive salad which is particularly good with poultry, pork or ham.

1 lb (450 g) small young turnips
1 tblsp sesame oil
1 tblsp soy sauce
1 tblsp cider vinegar
1 tsp caster sugar
pinch of ground ginger

1. Peel the turnips and slice them very thinly. Place in a serving bowl.

2. Mix together the oil, sauce, vinegar, sugar and ginger. Pour over the turnips and leave to stand for 4 hours before serving.

MIXED SALADS

Pizza Salad

A hot salad which makes the perfect accompaniment to cold meats or fish, but can be used as a simple meal on its own with wholemeal bread.

5 large tomatoes
1 small onion
2 tblsp olive oil
1 tblsp wine vinegar
1 tsp dried marjoram
salt and pepper
pinch of sugar
6 oz (150 g) Cheddar or Mozzarella cheese
8 green or black olives
2 oz (50 g) anchovy fillets

1. Slice the tomatoes thickly and place in an oiled ovenware dish.

2. Slice the onions thinly and break into rings. Put into boiling water and simmer for 5 minutes. Drain well and arrange on tomatoes.

3. Beat oil, vinegar, marjoram, salt, pepper and sugar together and pour into the dish.

4. Slice the cheese thinly and arrange on top of the onions. Garnish with halved olives and drained anchovies.

5. Bake at 375°F (109° C), Gas 5 for 30 minutes. Serve hot.

Peperonata

This is delicious hot or cold as a first course (with crusty bread) or as a side salad.

4 large red or green peppers
6 large tomatoes
2 oz (50 g) butter
2 tblsp olive oil
1 medium onion
1 garlic clove, crushed
salt
1 tblsp chopped fresh basil

1. Halve the peppers and remove seeds. Cut the flesh into strips.

2. Skin the tomatoes and chop roughly.

3. Heat the butter and oil together and add finely sliced onion. Cook gently until the onion is soft and golden.

4. Add the peppers, cover and simmer for 15 minutes.

5. Add tomatoes, garlic and salt. Cook until the tomatoes and peppers are soft and the oil is absorbed, leaving a fairly dry mixture.

6. Place in serving dish and sprinkle with basil. Serve hot or cold.

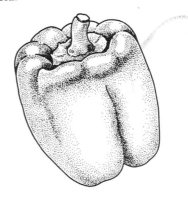

Ratatouille

Serve hot or cold as a side salad, or as a separate course with crusty white bread, or wholemeal rolls.

2 medium aubergines
1 green pepper
2 medium onions
2 courgettes
1 lb (450 g) tomatoes
¼ pint (150 ml) olive oil
1 garlic clove, crushed
salt and pepper
1 tblsp chopped fresh parsley

1. Do not peel aubergines, but slice them into 1 in (2.5 cm) slices.

2. Cut the pepper in half, remove seeds, and chop the flesh coarsely.

3. Chop the onions coarsely. Slice the unpeeled courgettes.

4. Skin the tomatoes and slice them.

5. Heat the oil and add the aubergines, pepper, onions and courgettes. Cover and simmer for 20 minutes.

6. Add the tomatoes, garlic, salt and pepper. Stir well, cover tightly and simmer for 1 hour, until the vegetables are cooked and the oil has been absorbed.

7. Sprinkle with parsley and serve hot or cold.

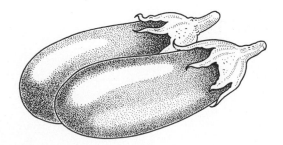

Red and Green Salad

A pleasant change from the traditional green salad, using some of the less usual ingredients now available.

1 head chicory
½ head curly endive
1 head Florence fennel (finocchio)
1 small head red chicory (radiccio)
8 radishes
5 tblsp olive oil
2 tblsp red wine vinegar
salt and pepper

1. Slice the chicory across in thin rings.

2. Divide the curly endive into leaves and arrange in a salad bowl.

3. Cut the fennel in quarters and then slice each quarter thinly. Mix the fennel and chicory and arrange on the endive leaves.

4. Tear the red chicory leaves into small pieces, and place in the bowl.

5. Slice the radishes thinly and sprinkle on top of the salad.

6. Mix the oil and vinegar and season well with salt and pepper. Pour over the salad. Toss and serve at once.

Midwinter Health Salad

All winter vegetables are delicious eaten raw in salad, and this is a colourful and filling mixture.

8 oz (225 g) hard white cabbage
8 oz (225 g) red cabbage
10 Brussels sprouts
2 celery sticks
1 medium leek
2 medium carrots
8 tblsp oil
3 tblsp wine vinegar
pinch of mustard powder
salt and pepper

1. Shred the white and red cabbages very finely. Put into a large serving bowl.

2. Remove any discoloured leaves from the sprouts and cut the sprouts across in very thin slices. Add to the cabbage.

3. Clean the celery and leek and cut them across in very thin slices.

4. Grate the carrots coarsely. Add celery, leek and carrots to the bowl.

5. Mix the oil, vinegar, mustard, salt and pepper. Just before serving, pour over the salad and toss well.

Winter Health Salad

Crisp salad makes a welcome addition to heavy winter meals, and the fruit and nuts give added flavour and texture.

8 oz (225 g) cottage cheese
4 celery sticks
salt and pepper
chicory or watercress
2 oranges
12 cooked prunes
2 oz (50 g) chopped mixed nuts
1 tblsp chopped fresh parsley

1. Place the cottage cheese in a bowl. Chop the celery finely and mix with the cheese. Season well with salt and pepper.

2. Arrange chicory or watercress on a serving dish and place cheese mixture on top.

3. Peel the oranges and remove pith. Cut into crosswise slices and then halve the slices. Arrange round the cottage cheese.

4. Put prunes on the orange slices. Sprinkle nuts and parsley over cheese.

Crunchy Winter Salad

This salad is so filling that its almost a meal in itself. It is good for buffet meals when a selection of cold meat is being served.

12 oz (350 g) hard white cabbage
6 oz (150 g) carrots
1 green pepper
1 small onion
1 eating apple
1 tblsp lemon juice
2 oz (50 g) sultanas
2 oz (50 g) chopped mixed nuts
¼ pint (150 ml) mayonnaise

1. Shred the cabbage finely and place in a salad bowl.

2. Grate the carrots coarsely and mix with the cabbage.

3. Chop the green pepper and onion finely and sprinkle in the bowl.

4. Leave the skin on the apple, but remove the core and dice the flesh. Sprinkle well with lemon juice, and add to the salad bowl.

5. Sprinkle on the sultanas and nuts.

6. Add the mayonnaise and toss the salad well. Chill slightly before serving.

Mixed Green Salad

While a green salad may consist of nothing but lettuce tossed in an oil and vinegar dressing, the flavour is greatly enhanced by a few watercress leaves, perhaps some thin slices of cucumber, or some other green leaves such as curly endive. A sprinkling of mixed fresh herbs gives a little extra colour and flavour.

1 crisp lettuce
½ bunch watercress
4 oz (100 g) cucumber
French Dressing (p. 82)
1 tblsp chopped fresh mixed herbs

1. Wash the lettuce thoroughly and dry in a salad basket, or pat dry lightly with a cloth or kitchen paper.

2. Tear the leaves (do not cut) into bite-sized pieces and place in a serving bowl.

3. Break the watercress into small sprigs and add to the lettuce.

4. Peel the cucumber and cut the flesh into thin slices. Add to the bowl.

5. Just before serving, pour over the dressing and toss lightly. Sprinkle with herbs and serve at once.

*If the flavour of garlic is liked, rub the salad bowl with a cut garlic clove before putting in the lettuce leaves.

Sweet and Sharp Salad

The raisins and lemon juice give a special flavour to this simple salad made from everyday ingredients.

4 medium carrots
4 oz (100 g) cucumber
2 oz (50 g) seedless raisins
2 tblsp lemon juice
1 tsp olive oil
½ tsp chopped fresh mixed herbs
salt and pepper

1. Grate the carrots coarsely and put into a salad bowl.

2. Peel the cucumber and cut into small dice. Mix with the carrots and raisins.

3. Combine lemon juice, oil, herbs, salt and pepper. Pour over salad and mix gently.

Ploughman's Salad

This is a very old-fashioned salad from Yorkshire, in which the unusual dressing makes bland lettuce more interesting.

1 lettuce
2 tblsp finely chopped fresh chives
2 tblsp malt vinegar
1 tblsp black treacle
salt and pepper

1. Shred the lettuce finely and place in a salad bowl. Mix with the chives.

2. Mix the vinegar and treacle and season well with salt and pepper.

3. Just before serving, pour the dressing into the bowl and toss the lettuce.

Hot Green Salad

Hot bacon fat is often used in Europe and America to dress and flavour green salads. This type of salad is delicious with cold meats.

3 oz (75 g) bacon fat
1 small onion
4 oz (100 g) fresh young spinach
1 lettuce
salt and pepper
1 tblsp wine vinegar

1. Heat the bacon fat in a thick pan. Chop the onion very finely and cook gently for 2 minutes.

2. Wash and dry the spinach and lettuce. Shred the leaves finely into a bowl.

3. Add the spinach and lettuce to the bacon fat. Heat until the leaves are wilted.

4. Season well and sprinkle with vinegar. Turn into serving bowl and serve at once.

Vegetable Macedoine Salad

A useful mixture of cooked vegetables which may be made with leftovers. If cooked beetroot is added, it is commonly known as "Russian salad".

8 oz (225 g) cooked French beans
4 oz (100 g) cooked peas
1 large cooked carrot
3 celery sticks
4 oz (100 g) asparagus tips (optional)
¼ pint (150 ml) mayonnaise

1. Cut the beans into small neat chunks and mix with the peas.

2. Dice the carrot and add to the bowl.

3. Cut the celery into thin slices and add to the other vegetables. Add pieces of asparagus if available.

4. Pour on the mayonnaise and mix well. Chill for 30 minutes before serving.

Summer Salad Dip

This can be just as good in colder weather if crunchy winter vegetables are used such as celery or chicory. Choose the ingredients according to whatever is available in good condition. Cheese biscuits or crisps may be added if liked.

cucumber
carrots
red or green peppers
button mushrooms
radishes
spring onions
chicory
cauliflower florets
celery sticks
4 tblsp mayonnaise
2 tblsp tomato ketchup
4 tsp made mustard

1. Prepare vegetables so that they can be easily handled e.g. cucumber strips, carrot strips, pepper fingers, single chicory leaves.

2. Place vegetables in a bowl of water with ice cubes until serving time.

3. Mix together mayonnaise, tomato ketchup and mustard and place in a bowl in the centre of a serving dish.

4. Drain and dry vegetables well and arrange around the bowl of sauce. If liked, add small cheese biscuits, crisps, fingers of crispbread or breadsticks.

RICE, PASTA AND PULSES

Haricot Bean Salad

Small pieces of cooked lamb may be added to this salad to make a complete meal.

8 oz (225 g) dried haricot beans
¼ pint (150 ml) olive oil
2 medium onions
2 garlic cloves, crushed
1 bay leaf
pinch of thyme
2 tsp concentrated tomato purée
salt and pepper
juice of 1 lemon
2 tblsp chopped fresh parsley

1. Soak the beans in water overnight, and drain.

2. Heat the oil in a pan and add 1 finely chopped onion. Cook over low heat until soft and golden.

3. Add the beans, garlic, bay leaf, thyme and tomato purée. Cook gently for 10 minutes.

4. Add enough boiling water to cover the beans by 1 inch (2.5 cm). Simmer for about 2 hours until tender, when the water should have been absorbed.

5. Season well with salt and pepper and stir in lemon juice.

6. Place in serving dish and sprinkle with parsley. Slice the remaining onion thinly and place on top of the salad.

Red Bean Salad

Canned cooked beans may be used to speed up the preparation. They should be drained and mixed with the dressing.

1 lb (450 g) red kidney beans
3 tblsp olive oil
1 tblsp wine vinegar
1 garlic clove crushed
pinch of mustard powder
pinch of tarragon
salt and pepper
3 tomatoes
1 small onion

1. Rinse the beans and cover them with cold water. Bring to the boil and boil for 2 minutes. Remove from heat and leave to stand for 1 hour.

2. Bring back to the boil and simmer for 1 hour until tender but not broken. Drain very thoroughly.

3. Mix the oil, vinegar, garlic, mustard, tarragon, salt and pepper in a jug and pour over the hot beans. Leave until cool.

4. Skin the tomatoes, remove the seeds and chop the flesh roughly.

5. Chop the onion finely.

6. Mix the tomatoes and onion with the beans. Serve cold but not chilled.

Chick Pea Salad

This may be eaten as a first course with wholemeal bread. It is a good side dish to serve with a spicy food such as curry.

1 lb (450 g) chick peas
1 medium onion
1 garlic clove, crushed
1 tblsp olive oil
1 tblsp lemon juice
salt and black pepper
3 tblsp chopped fresh parsley

1. Soak the chick peas overnight in cold water until doubled in bulk.

2. Drain and place in saucepan. Cover with water about 2 in (5 cm) over the peas.

3. Bring to the boil, skim, and simmer for 45 minutes until tender.

4. Chop the onion finely and mix with the garlic, oil, lemon juice, salt and pepper.

5. Drain the chick peas thoroughly. Toss in the dressing and leave until cold.

6. Sprinkle with more freshly-ground pepper and with parsley.

Bean and Lamb Salad

A good second-day dish when the remains of a lamb joint have to be eaten. For speed, the salad may be made with a can of butter beans.

8 oz (225 g) butter beans
8 oz (225 g) cooked lamb
2 eating apples
3 tblsp mayonnaise
1 tsp curry powder
4 oz (100 g) red cabbage

1. Cook the beans in boiling salted water until tender but not broken. Drain well and place in a bowl.

2. Cube the cooked lamb and mix with the beans.

3. Do not peel the apple but remove core and dice the flesh roughly. Mix with the beans and lamb.

4. Mix the mayonnaise with curry powder. Add to the beans and mix well.

5. Shred the cabbage finely and arrange on a serving dish. Top with the bean and lamb mixture.

Mexican Coleslaw

A variation on traditional Coleslaw with kidney beans and a light dressing which is full of flavour.

12 oz (350 g) hard white cabbage
6 oz (150 g) canned kidney beans
1 medium onion
3 tblsp mayonnaise
1 tsp lemon juice
pinch of fennel seeds

1. Shred the cabbage finely and put into a salad bowl.

2. Drain the beans well and mix with the cabbage.

3. Chop the onion very finely and add to the bowl.

4. Mix the mayonnaise and lemon juice and pour into the bowl. Toss the salad lightly. Sprinkle with fennel seeds.

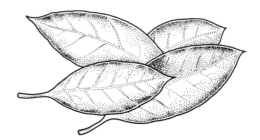

Lentil Salad

A well-seasoned salad which is filling enough for a complete meal, or a perfect accompaniment to curries.

1 lb (450 g) lentils
3 pints (1.8 l) water
2 bay leaves
1 large onion
4 cloves
salt and pepper
½ tsp mustard powder
½ tsp paprika
6 spring onions
4 oz (100 g) dill pickled cucumbers
5 tblsp olive oil
3 tblsp wine vinegar
3 tblsp chopped fresh parsley

1. Soak lentils in the water for 4 hours. Put into a pan with the water, bay leaves, chopped onion, cloves, salt and pepper. Cover and bring to the boil. Simmer until the lentils are just tender but not mushy. Drain well and discard bay leaves, onions and cloves

2. Put into a bowl and mix with the mustard, paprika, finely chopped spring onions and cucumbers.

3. Mix the oil and vinegar. Pour over the lentils and toss lightly.

4. Sprinkle thickly with the parsley.

Hot Bean Salad

This simple hot salad makes a good first course, or a main meal with wholemeal bread.

1 lb (450 g) haricot beans
3 medium onions
4 tblsp olive oil
6 anchovy fillets
salt and pepper
pinch of ground nutmeg
juice of 1 lemon
1 tblsp chopped fresh parsley

1. Soak the beans overnight in cold water. Drain well, cover with fresh water and bring slowly to the boil. Boil for about 1½ hours until tender. Drain and reserve the liquid.

2. Chop the onions finely and cook gently in the oil until soft and golden.

3. Add chopped anchovies, salt, pepper, nutmeg, lemon juice and 8 tablespoons cooking liquid. Simmer for 5 minutes.

4. Pour mixture over the beans and serve hot, sprinkled with parsley.

Bean Sprout and Mushroom Salad

The mushrooms should not be peeled, but just wiped with kitchen paper before slicing. If possible, use a mixture of sprouts, but otherwise one type may be used if a variety is not available.

6 oz (150 g) button mushrooms
3 oz (75 g) Chinese bean sprouts
4 oz (100 g) alfalfa sprouts
4 tblsp salad oil
2 tblsp lemon juice
1 garlic clove, crushed
salt and pepper

1. Wipe the mushrooms and cut them across in thin slices.

2. Mix with the bean sprouts and alfalfa sprouts.

3. Mix together the oil, lemon juice, garlic and plenty of salt and pepper.

4. Pour over the salad and leave to stand for 1 hour before serving.

Chinese Salad

This makes a refreshing first course, or may be used as a side salad. The nuts and seeds give a crunchy texture.

4 oz (100 g) Chinese bean sprouts
2 celery sticks
1 large carrot
8 oz (225 g) canned mandarin oranges
2 oz (50 g) cashew nuts
1 tblsp sesame seeds
4 tblsp salad oil
2 tblsp lemon juice
watercress or lettuce leaves

1. Place the bean sprouts in a bowl.

2. Chop the celery finely. Grate the carrot coarsely. Add to the bean sprouts.

3. Drain the mandarin oranges and add to the sprouts. Add the nuts and sesame seeds.

4. Mix the oil and lemon juice and pour over the salad.

5. Arrange a bed of watercress or lettuce on a serving dish. Place the salad in the centre.

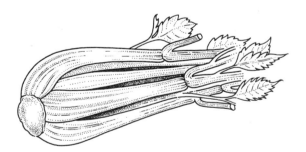

Whole Earth Salad

The cheese makes this a complete meal, but it may be omitted if only vegetables are preferred.

3 oz (75 g) Chinese bean sprouts
3 oz (75 g) adzuki bean sprouts
3 oz (75 g) alfalfa sprouts
4 oz (100 g) Cheddar cheese
1 well-hearted lettuce
1 green pepper
3 spring onions
2 tblsp chopped fresh parsley
2 large tomatoes
1 avocado
6 tblsp salad oil
2 tblsp wine vinegar

1. Stir the three kinds of sprouts together in a bowl.

2. Cut the cheese into small cubes and add to the sprouts.

3. Tear the lettuce into small pieces and add to the salad.

4. Remove the seeds from the pepper and chop the flesh finely. Add to the bowl.

5. Add the finely chopped onions and parsley.

6. Skin the tomatoes and remove seeds. Chop the flesh coarsely and add to the salad.

7. Peel the avocado and slice the flesh into small pieces. Add to the salad.

8. Mix the oil and vinegar and pour into the bowl. Mix well and serve at once.

Danish Chef's Salad (page 60)

Rice and Vegetable Salad

A mixture of rice and colourful vegetables which can be used as a light meal or as an accompaniment to meat or fish.

8 oz (225 g) long grain rice
8 oz (225 g) shelled fresh or frozen peas
4 oz (100 g) sweetcorn kernels
4 oz (100 g) button mushrooms
1 small red pepper
2 celery sticks
¼ pint (150 ml) natural yoghurt
1 tblsp chopped fresh mixed herbs
salt and pepper

1. Cook rice in boiling salted water for 12 minutes until just tender. Drain well, rinse in cold water, and place in salad bowl.

2. Cook the peas in boiling salted water for 15 minutes if fresh, or for 5 minutes if frozen. Drain well and mix with rice.

3. Add the sweetcorn kernels.

4. Wipe the mushrooms and slice them finely. Add to the bowl.

5. Chop the red pepper and celery finely and mix into bowl.

6. Beat together the yoghurt, herbs, salt and pepper. Pour over the salad and toss just before serving.

Venetian Rice Salad

The Venetians have a traditional dish which is a mixture of rice and peas. This salad version is enhanced with prawns.

8 oz (225 g) brown rice
1 pint (600 ml) chicken stock
1 lb (450 g) shelled (or frozen) peas
4 oz (100 g) butter
1 small onion
1 tsp honey
pinch of nutmeg
salt and pepper
1 tsp chopped fresh basil or tarragon
8 oz (225 g) peeled prawns
4 tblsp olive oil
1 tblsp chopped fresh chives

1. Cook the rice in boiling stock until tender, adding a little water if the liquid evaporates. Drain and leave to cool in a salad bowl.

2. If frozen peas are used, let them thaw before cooking. Melt the butter in a thick pan and cook the finely chopped onion until soft and golden. Add the peas, honey, nutmeg, salt and pepper. Pour in 8 tablespoons water, cover tightly and cook very gently until tender. Drain off any surplus liquid. Stir in the basil or tarragon and leave until cold.

3. Mix the peas into the rice and stir in the prawns. Add the oil and toss lightly.

4. Sprinkle with chives and serve at once.

American Cheese and Fruit Salad (page 61)

Fruited Rice Salad

A complete meal in which the sweet fruit contrasts with the slight saltiness of the meat and the texture of the rice.

8 oz (225 g) patna rice
8 oz (225 g) thickly sliced cooked tongue
2 eating pears
8 oz (225 g) canned pineapple chunks
juice of 1 lemon
lettuce leaves
¼ pint (150 ml) mayonnaise
¼ pint (150 ml) whipping cream

1. Cook the rice in the boiling salted water for 12 minutes. Drain well, rinse in cold water and drain again.

2. Cut the tongue in small cubes and mix with the rice.

3. Peel the pears and dice the flesh. Mix with drained pineapple and stir into the rice. Sprinkle with lemon juice.

4. Arrange a bed of lettuce leaves in a serving bowl and spoon the rice mixture into the bowl.

5. Put the mayonnaise into a bowl. Whip the cream to soft peaks and fold into the mayonnaise. Serve separately.

Golden Rice Salad

Cooking the rice in tea with turmeric gives the grains a beautiful golden colour, while the anchovies and bacon add piquancy.

¾ pint (450 ml) tea (without milk)
6 oz (150 g) long grain rice
½ tsp turmeric
½ tsp salt
2 oz (50 g) canned anchovies
2 oz (50 g) back bacon
2 oz (50 g) peanuts
2 celery sticks
1 small onion
1 red pepper

1. Bring the tea to the boil and add the rice, turmeric and salt. Boil for 12 minutes until tender. Drain, rinse in cold water, and place in serving bowl.

2. Drain anchovies, chop and add to the rice.

3. Grill the bacon until crisp. Chop in small pieces and add to the rice.

4. Use fat which has run from the bacon for lightly frying the peanuts. Drain and stir into the rice.

5. Chop the celery, onion and green pepper finely. Stir into the salad bowl.

Green Rice Salad

A pretty salad with a nice mixture of textures. Chinese bean or adzuki bean sprouts may be substituted for the fenugreek.

8 oz (225 g) long grain rice
2 oz (50 g) fenugreek sprouts
bunch of watercress
2 tblsp chopped fresh parsley
2 tblsp chopped fresh chives
4 tblsp olive or salad oil
2 tblsp wine vinegar
salt and pepper

1. Cook the rice in boiling salted water for 12 minutes until just tender. Rinse well in cold water, drain and leave until cold.

2. Put the rice into a serving bowl and stir in the fenugreek sprouts. Add the watercress leaves, parsley and chives.

3. Mix the oil, vinegar, salt and pepper. Pour over the salad and toss well.

Rice Slaw

This is a good winter salad mixture with plenty of texture and flavour.

8 oz (225 g) long grain rice
12 oz (350 g) hard white cabbage
2 medium carrots
1 small green pepper
2 oz (50 g) sultanas
6 tblsp salad oil
2 tblsp wine vinegar
salt and pepper

1. Cook rice in boiling salted water for 12 minutes until just tender. Drain well, rinse in cold water and place in salad bowl.

2. Shred the cabbage finely and add to bowl.

3. Grate the carrots coarsely and mix with the cabbage and rice.

4. Chop the green pepper finely and add to bowl. Add the sultanas.

5. Mix the oil, vinegar, salt and pepper. Just before serving, pour over salad and toss well.

Provençal Rice Salad

A delicious fish salad which makes a substantial meal.

1 medium onion, peeled
salt and pepper
½ tsp thyme
1 bay leaf
1 lb (450 g) cod fillets
1 pint (500 ml) water
¼ tsp saffron
8oz (225 g) long grain rice
1 tsp salt
10 black and 10 green olives
1 can anchovy fillets
¼ pint (125 ml) mayonnaise
4 tomatoes, quartered
½ lettuce, shredded

1. Put the onion in a large saucepan with the salt, pepper, thyme, bay leaf and cold water.

2. Bring to the boil and add the fish. Bring back to the boil and when the water is boiling, remove from the heat and allow the fish to cool in the cooking liquid.

3. Bring the water to a boil and add the saffron, rice and salt. Boil for 12 minutes until tender. Drain, rinse in cold water, and place in a bowl.

4. Mix the rice, olives, anchovies (cut in two), mayonnaise and tomatoes. Drain the cooked fish, break into large pieces and add to rice. Mix gently.

5. Cover and chill for 1 hour. Just before serving add the lettuce and mix.

Curried Rice Salad

Curry and rice naturally go together, and this delicious salad is the perfect accompaniment to poultry.

2 oz (50 g) seedless raisins
8 oz (225 g) patna rice
1½ tblsp curry powder
1 eating apple
1 tblsp lemon juice
½ pint (300 ml) mayonnaise

1. Put the raisins into a small bowl. Cover with boiling water and leave to stand for 1 hour until the raisins are plump. Drain well.

2. Cook rice in boiling salted water for 5 minutes. Add the curry powder and continue cooking for 12 minutes until the rice is just tender. Drain well, rinse in cold water and drain again.

3. Mix rice and raisins in a serving bowl.

4. Do not peel the apple, but remove the core and chop the flesh into small chunks. Sprinkle with lemon juice.

5. Stir the apple chunks into the rice and then stir in the mayonnaise. Chill for 30 minutes before serving.

Pasta Niçoise

The addition of pasta makes a traditional Niçoise salad
more substantial.

8 oz (225 g) pasta shells
4 hardboiled eggs
4 large tomatoes
1 red pepper
4 oz (100 g) cooked French beans
7 oz (200 g) canned tuna
8 black olives
1 tsp capers
4 tblsp olive oil
2 tblsp wine vinegar
1 garlic clove, crushed
salt and pepper

1. Cook the pasta in boiling salted water for 10-12
   minutes until tender but not broken. Drain well and
   rinse in cold water.

2. Cut the eggs in lengthwise quarters. Quarter the
   tomatoes.

3. Remove seeds from the red pepper and cut the flesh
   into thin slices.

4. Cut the beans in chunks.

5. Drain the tuna and break the flesh into chunks.

6. Mix together the pasta, eggs, pepper, tomatoes, beans
   and tuna in a serving bowl. Add the olives and
   capers.

7. Mix the oil, vinegar, garlic, salt and pepper, and pour
   over the salad. Toss well just before serving.

COMPLETE MEAL
SALADS

German Tongue Salad

This salad makes a most attractive main dish when arranged decoratively on a platter.

12 oz (350 g) cooked tongue
4 tblsp olive oil
1½ tblsp white wine vinegar
½ tsp mustard powder
2 tsp capers
1 tblsp chopped fresh parsley
salt and pepper
2 cooked beetroot
8 oz (225 g) cooked new potatoes (or small old ones)
2 hardboiled eggs

1. Cut the tongue into short, narrow strips and place in a bowl.

2. Mix the oil, vinegar, mustard, chopped capers, parsley, salt and pepper. Pour over the tongue and leave to stand for 3 hours.

3. Slice the beetroot thinly and arrange around the edge of a serving dish.

4. Arrange whole potatoes in another circle inside the beetroot.

5. Pile the tongue in the centre with any surplus dressing.

6. Garnish with roughly-chopped eggs.

Herring and Apple Salad

A tasty salad which makes a good first course or complete meal, accompanied by rye bread, pumpernickel or wholemeal bread.

12 oz (350 g) rollmop herring
3 eating apples
12 oz (350 g) cold boiled potatoes
1 medium cooked beetroot
1 small onion
3 tblsp mayonnaise
3 tblsp sour cream
salt and pepper
lettuce leaves
1 tblsp chopped fresh parsley

1. Drain the herrings and cut into strips.

2. Leave the skins on the apples but remove the cores. Cut into cubes.

3. Dice the potatoes and the beetroot. Grate the onion finely.

4. Mix together herrings, apples, potatoes, beetroot and onion.

5. Mix together the mayonnaise and sour cream, and season with salt and pepper. Pour over the salad and toss lightly.

6. Arrange lettuce leaves in a salad bowl and spoon the salad into the middle. Sprinkle chopped parsley on top.

Russian Salad

A traditional Russian salad contains meat or fish as well as cooked vegetables mixed with raw salad ingredients.

2 large cooked beetroot
12 oz (350 g) cooked potatoes
8 oz (225 g) ham
1 large dill-pickled cucumber
1 eating apple
1 tblsp finely chopped onion
4 oz (100 g) cooked peas
6 tblsp salad oil
3 tblsp wine vinegar
1 garlic clove, crushed
salt and pepper
lettuce leaves
watercress
mayonnaise

1. Dice the beetroot, potatoes, ham and cucumber and mix in a bowl.

2. Peel and core the apple. Dice the flesh and add to the salad with the onion and peas.

3. Mix together the oil, vinegar, garlic, salt and pepper. Pour over the salad and mix well.

4. Arrange lettuce leaves on a serving plate and spoon on the salad. Garnish with the watercress and place a few spoonfuls of mayonnaise in the centre of the salad.

Pineapple and Shrimp Salad

A wonderful mixture of textures and refreshing flavours which makes a colourful summer salad.

2 small pineapples
8 oz (225 g) peeled shrimps or prawns
8 oz (225 g) cooked French beans
½ cucumber
½ pint (300 ml) mayonnaise
1 tsp minced onion
1 tsp curry powder

1. Cut the pineapples in half lengthwise, leaving the leaves on top. Cut out the flesh carefully, leaving a neat shell. Remove hard core and dice the soft flesh. Place in a bowl.

2. Add the shrimps or prawns and chopped beans to the pineapple.

3. Peel the cucumber and remove the seeds. Dice the flesh and add to the pineapple.

4. Mix the mayonnaise with the onion and curry powder. Pour over the contents of the bowl.

5. Divide mixture between the pineapple shells and chill for 30 minutes before serving so that the flavours blend.

Italian Salad

A substantial salad which can be a complete meal, and is very good if accompanied by sliced tomatoes, watercress and crusty bread.

8 oz (225 g) short macaroni
1 small minced onion
4 oz (100 g) cottage cheese
¼ pint (150 ml) natural yoghurt
2 oz (50 g) anchovy fillets
salt and pepper
1 tblsp grated Parmesan cheese
6 black or green olives

1. Cook the macaroni in boiling salted water until tender. Drain well and rinse under hot water. Place in a bowl.

2. Stir in the onion.

3. Sieve the cottage cheese. Add to the bowl with the yoghurt and mix well. Leave until just cold.

4. Chop the anchovies and stir into the mixture, and season to taste with salt and pepper.

5. Just before serving, sprinkle with Parmesan cheese and garnish with olives.

Rice and Chicken Salad

A light but filling meal, which also makes an excellent buffet dish accompanied by other salads. Ham may be used instead of chicken.

8 oz (225 g) long grain rice
1 garlic clove
4 tblsp salad oil
2 tblsp wine vinegar
salt and pepper
2 oz (50 g) seedless raisins
1 green pepper
2 large tomatoes
1 lb (450 g) cooked chicken

1. Cook rice in boiling salted water for 12 minutes until just tender. Drain well and rinse in cold water.

2. Cut the garlic in pieces and rub round a salad bowl.

3. Mix oil, vinegar, salt and pepper. Add raisins.

4. Dice the green pepper. Skin, seed and chop the tomatoes. Mix pepper and tomatoes with the dressing.

5. Add dressing to rice and mix well.

6. Place diced chicken on top of salad and mix again.

French Seafood Salad

A delicious mixture of fish and raw vegetables with a special paprika-flavoured mayonnaise.

1 lettuce
1 lb (450 g) button mushrooms
3 tblsp lemon juice
1 lb (450 g) tomatoes
3 hardboiled eggs
8 oz (225 g) can tuna in brine
8 oz (225 g) peeled prawns
2 tblsp olive oil
1 tblsp wine vinegar
salt and pepper
½ pint (300 ml) mayonnaise
½ oz (15 g) paprika

1. Shred the lettuce and place in a large serving bowl.

2. Wipe the mushrooms but do not peel them. Trim the stems and cut the mushrooms into thin slices and place in a bowl. Add the lemon juice, stir well, and leave to stand while the rest of the salad is prepared.

3. Skin the tomatoes and cut them into quarters. Cut the eggs into lengthwise quarters. Place on the bed of lettuce.

4. Drain the tuna and break into chunks. Add to the bowl, with the prawns. Sprinkle on the mushrooms.

5. Mix the oil, vinegar, salt and pepper and pour over the salad. Mix gently so that the eggs do not break.

6. Stir the paprika into a little of the mayonnaise until completely blended. Work in the remaining mayonnaise and place in a serving bowl.

Smoked Haddock and Bean Salad

The mixture of smoked fish with beans and a curry dressing makes a very tasty meal, accompanied by wholemeal bread.

1 lb (450 g) smoked haddock
milk and water
1 lb (450 g) cooked butter beans
¼ pint (150 ml) natural yoghurt
2 tblsp lemon juice
1 tblsp chopped fresh parsley
2 tsp curry powder
salt and pepper
1 lettuce
1 hardboiled egg

1. Put the fish into a shallow pan and just cover with milk and water. Poach over low heat for 10 minutes and drain well. Remove skin and bones and flake fish with a fork.

2. Mix the fish and butter beans in a bowl.

3. Mix the yoghurt, lemon juice, parsley, curry powder, salt and pepper. Pour over the fish and beans and mix well.

4. Arrange a bed of lettuce on serving dish. Spoon on the fish mixture. Garnish with sliced egg.

Chef's Salad Bowl

A favourite restaurant suggestion for a light meal which is easily adapted for family occasions.

1 lettuce
8 spinach leaves
1 small cucumber
8 radishes
½ bunch watercress
8 small tomatoes
4 oz (100 g) sliced ham
2 oz (50 g) sliced tongue
2 oz (50 g) sliced turkey or chicken
2 oz (50 g) sliced garlic sausage
4 oz (100 g) Gruyère cheese
8 tblsp French Dressing (p. 82)

1. Tear the lettuce and spinach leaves into bite-sized pieces and place in salad bowl.

2. Slice the cucumber and radishes thinly, and add to the bowl.

3. Chop the watercress and put into the bowl.

4. Cut the tomatoes into quarters and add to the salad.

5. Cut all the meats and cheese into matchstick pieces and add to the bowl.

6. Just before serving, pour on dressing and toss well.

Danish Chef's Salad

A simple mixed salad made with two of Denmark's most famous products — bacon and blue cheese — which forms an easily-made complete meal.

8 oz (225 g) cooked gammon
4 oz (100 g) Danish Blue cheese
1 cos lettuce
1 bunch radishes
2 ins (5 cm) cucumber
1 medium onion
6 tblsp French Dressing (p. 82)

1. Cut gammon into medium-thick strips.

2. Cut the cheese into small cubes.

3. Shred the lettuce. Slice the radishes and cucumber. Slice the onion into thin rings.

4. Arrange the salad ingredients in alternate layers in a serving bowl.

5. Pour on the dressing just before serving.

Cheese and Apple Salad

A good winter mixture which makes a complete and nourishing meal.

4 oz (100 g) Cheddar cheese
4 eating apples
2 tblsp lemon juice
6 celery sticks
6 canned pineapple rings
6 tblsp mayonnaise
lettuce or chicory leaves

1. Dice the cheese into small cubes and put into a bowl.

2. Do not peel the apples, but core and chop the flesh. Sprinkle with lemon juice.

3. Chop the celery and pineapple rings.

4. Mix the cheese, apples and lemon juice, celery, pineapple and mayonnaise. Chill for 30 minutes.

5. Arrange lettuce or chicory leaves on a serving dish. Pile the cheese mixture on top and serve immediately.

American Cheese and Fruit Salad

Fruit preserved in its own juice has a particularly rich and delicious flavour which is combined here with crisp salad and tasty cheese.

15¼ oz (432 g) canned pineapple slices in own juice
1 banana
1 eating apple
4 celery sticks
½ Webb's or Iceberg lettuce
½ bunch radishes
6 oz (150 g) Cheddar cheese
¼ pint (150 ml) Danish Blue Cheese Dressing (p. 83)

1. Drain the pineapple, reserving the juice. Cut into small pieces.

2. Slice the banana. Do not peel the apple, but core it and dice the flesh. Moisten fruit with pineapple juice to prevent browning.

3. Slice the celery thinly. Shred the lettuce finely. Slice the radishes. Mix fruit and vegetables together.

4. Cut the Cheddar cheese in cubes and mix into the salad.

5. Pour over the dressing and toss lightly just before serving.

Party Fish Salad

A delicious low-calorie salad which is good for a buffet party, or which may be used as a first course.

1 lb (450 g) cod or haddock fillet
1 small onion
¼ pint (150 ml) white wine
4 oz (100 g) smoked salmon
4 oz (100 g) white grapes
3 celery sticks
3 tblsp salad oil
1 tblsp lemon juice
salt and pepper
watercress sprigs

1. Skin the fish and cut the flesh into cubes.

2. Chop the onion finely. Poach the fish and onion in white wine for 5 minutes. Drain and cool.

3. Cut the smoked salmon into small pieces. Halve and seed the grapes. Slice the celery thinly.

4. Mix the oil, lemon juice, salt and pepper.

5. Mix all the ingredients gently in a serving dish. Garnish with watercress sprigs.

Pineapple Chicken Salad

A piquant salad in a light creamy dressing which makes a very good buffet dish.

1 lb (450 g) cooked chicken
8 oz (225 g) canned pineapple chunks
3 celery sticks
12 stuffed olives
¼ pint (150 ml) mayonnaise
6 tblsp double cream
1 tsp curry powder
1 tblsp redcurrant jelly
lettuce leaves

1. Dice the chicken meat and put into a bowl.

2. Drain the pineapple and cut each cube into four dice.

3. Slice the celery and olives finely. Mix with chicken and pineapple.

4. Mix the mayonnaise, cream and curry powder. Warm the redcurrant jelly until just melted and stir into the mayonnaise.

5. Arrange a bed of lettuce in a serving bowl. Arrange the chicken mixture in the bowl. Pour on the dressing and toss just before serving.

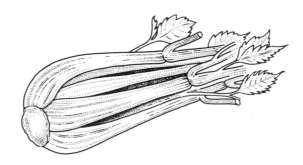

Niçoise Salad

A favourite salad which is a complete meal, and which may be slightly varied according to taste, but this recipe contains the traditional ingredients.

1 crisp lettuce
4 tomatoes
2 hardboiled eggs
4 oz (100 g) cucumber
4 oz (100 g) cooked French beans
1 green or red pepper
8 oz (225 g) canned tuna in brine or oil
2 oz (50 g) anchovy fillets
2 oz (50 g) black olives
¼ pint (150 ml) French Dressing (p.82)
mayonnaise

1. Wash the lettuce well and dry. Break into pieces and line a large salad bowl.

2. Skin the tomatoes and cut them in quarters (or eighths if large), and place in the bowl.

3. Do not peel the cucumber, but cut into dice and add to bowl with the French beans cut into chunks, and the chopped pepper.

4. Drain the tuna and break into large pieces. Add to the bowl.

5. Arrange anchovies and olives on top.

6. Just before serving, pour on the dressing and toss lightly.

7. Serve at once with additional mayonnaise if liked.

Seafood and Mushroom Salad

This makes a lovely summer meal if served with wholemeal bread and butter, but it can be a delicious first course if served in small portions. If scallops are unobtainable, the quantity of prawns may be doubled or trebled.

1 lb (450 g) button mushrooms
¼ pint (150 ml) olive oil
2 tblsp lemon juice
1 garlic clove
salt and pepper
8 scallops
4 oz (100 g) peeled prawns
2 tblsp chopped fresh parsley

1. Wipe the mushrooms and slice them thinly. Place in a serving bowl. Mix the oil, lemon juice, crushed garlic and seasoning, and pour half the mixture over the mushrooms. Leave to stand for 2-3 hours.

2. Simmer the scallops in a little water for 5 minutes, adding the red 'coral' of the fish during the last minute. Drain well and cut each scallop across in two rounds.

3. Mix the warm scallops and prawns and cover with remaining dressing.

4. Just before serving, mix the fish and mushrooms and any liquid. Sprinkle thickly with parsley.

American Rice Salad

The protein content of this salad may be varied to taste, but the mixture of chicken, ham and prawns is particularly delicious with melon.

4 oz (100 g) long grain rice
4 oz (100 g) cold cooked chicken
4 oz (100 g) cold cooked ham
4 oz (100 g) peeled prawns
8 oz (225 g) melon
½ pint (300 ml) mayonnaise
2 tsp curry powder
lettuce leaves
2 tsp chopped fresh chives

1. Cook the rice in boiling salted water for 12 minutes. Drain and rinse in cold water. Drain well and place in a bowl.

2. Dice the chicken and ham and add to the rice with the prawns.

3. Peel the melon and remove seeds. Dice the flesh and add to the rice.

4. Mix the mayonnaise with the curry powder. Pour into the bowl and mix well.

5. Line a salad bowl with lettuce leaves. Spoon in the rice mixture. Sprinkle on the chopped chives.

Greek Tomato Salad

Any hard white cheese is suitable for this salad, but a goat's cheese is preferable because of the unique flavour. Serve with plenty of crusty bread for a complete meal.

1 crisp lettuce
1 lb (450 g) tomatoes
8 oz (225 g) fetta cheese
4 oz (100 g) cucumber
12 black olives
¼ pint (150 ml) French Dressing (p.82)
2 tsp chopped fresh marjoram

1. Wash and dry the lettuce well. Tear into pieces and put into a salad bowl.

2. Slice the tomatoes thickly and place on the lettuce.

3. Break the cheese into bite-sized pieces and add to the bowl.

4. Peel the cucumber and dice the flesh. Mix with the olives and sprinkle on the salad.

5. Just before serving, pour on the dressing and toss well. Sprinkle with marjoram and serve.

FRUIT SALADS

Peach and Orange Salad

The mixture of sweet fruit and spicy dressing makes a lively accompaniment to cold ham, pork or chicken.

1 lettuce
1 eating apple
2 peaches
1 oz (25 g) almonds
2 tblsp salad oil
1 tblsp Worcestershire sauce
juice of 1 orange
grated rind of ½ orange
salt and pepper
watercress spriggs

1. Arrange lettuce leaves on a serving dish.

2. Prepare the dressing by mixing oil, sauce, orange juice and rind, salt and pepper.

3. Do not peel the apple, but cut into quarters and remove the core. Cut into thin slices, toss in dressing and arrange in a circle on the lettuce.

4. Skin the peaches and remove stones. Cut into slices, toss in dressing and arrange in the centre of the dish. Pour over the remaining dressing.

5. Toast the almonds lightly under the grill. Sprinkle on the salad and garnish with watercress sprigs. Serve at once.

Conference Salad

A good slimming meal to make with ripe eating pears, which may be accompanied by wholemeal bread.

4 ripe Conference pears
juice of ½ lemon
1 lb (450 g) cottage cheese
1 bunch watercress

1. Peel the pears and cut them in half. Scoop out the cores. Dip the pears in lemon juice to keep them white. Arrange on a serving dish.

2. Put the cottage cheese in a bowl. Remove leaves from half the watercress and mix the leaves with the cheese. Use this mixture to fill the cavities of the pears, and to spoon round them.

3. Garnish with remaining watercress sprigs.

Orange Salad

This is the classic accompaniment to roast or cold duck. Sometimes the oranges are mixed with thin onion rings.

4 large oranges
lettuce leaves
watercress sprigs
4 tblsp salad oil
4 tblsp wine vinegar
salt and pepper
pinch of sugar

1. Remove 3 or 4 strips of orange peel without any pith, and cut the peel in very fine shreds. Blanch in boiling water for 1 minute and drain well.

2. Peel the oranges and remove all pith. Cut oranges across in thin crosswise slices and remove any pips.

3. Place a bed of lettuce on a serving plate. Arrange orange slices on top (adding any juice which has run out of them) and garnish with watercress sprigs.

4. Mix together oil, vinegar, salt, pepper and sugar. Pour over the oranges, and garnish with shredded orange peel. Serve chilled.

Prune and Apple Salad

Prunes give a touch of sweetness to this crisp salad which may be made at any time of the year.

12 oz (350 g) hard white cabbage
2 medium carrots
4 oz (100 g) cauliflower florets
2 celery sticks
2 eating apples
1 red or green pepper
4 oz (100 g) cucumber
12 prunes, soaked
¼ pint (150 ml) mayonnaise
¼ pint (150 ml) sour cream
salt and pepper
1 tblsp chopped chives

1. Shred the cabbage finely. Grate the carrots coarsely. Mix the vegetables together in a serving bowl.

2. Blanch the cauliflower florets for 1 minute in boiling salted water. Drain, rinse in cold water, dry and add to bowl.

3. Add chopped celery, peeled chopped apples, sliced pepper, and diced peeled cucumber.

4. Snip the flesh from the prunes with scissors, and add to the salad.

5. Lightly beat together mayonnaise, sour cream, salt and pepper. Pour over the salad and toss lightly. Sprinkle with chopped chives.

Piquant Apricot Salad

This salad offsets the richness of fat meats such as ham, pork, duck and goose. Canned whole or half apricots may be used.

1 lb (450 g) can apricots in syrup
¼ pint (150 ml) dry white wine
2 tblsp white wine vinegar
6 white peppercorns
1 clove
1 oz (25 g) sugar

1. Drain the apricots and place in a serving dish.

2. Mix ¼ pint (150 ml) syrup from apricots with wine, vinegar, peppercorns, clove and sugar. Heat gently until sugar dissolves and then boil for 5 minutes.

3. Strain and pour over apricots. Chill before serving.

Grapes in Mustard Cream

A particularly delicious salad to serve with fish or chicken, which may be served on a bed of chicory, lettuce or watercress.

8 oz (225 g) black and white grapes
6 tblsp double cream
2 tblsp mayonnaise
1 tblsp made mustard

1. Cut the grapes in half and remove pips. Place in a serving dish.

2. Whip the cream to soft peaks. Fold in the mayonnaise and mustard.

3. Add the mustard cream to the grapes and fold in grapes gently until they are covered. Chill lightly before serving.

Golden Corn Salad

A mixture of golden fruit and vegetables makes an attractive summer dish. The addition of cottage cheese makes a complete meal.

4 oranges
6 medium carrots
12 oz (350 g) cooked sweetcorn kernels
1 lemon
4 canned pineapple rings
4 canned apricot halves

1. Peel oranges and remove pith. Cut oranges into crosswise slices.

2. Grate carrots coarsely.

3. Drain sweetcorn well and arrange in the centre of 4 plates.

4. Cut lemon in wedges. Arrange orange slices and lemon wedges round the sweetcorn. Sprinkle carrots round orange slices.

5. Place a pineapple ring on the top of each portion of sweetcorn. Put an apricot half on top of each pineapple ring.

Plum and Tarragon Salad

The sweetness of ripe plums complements the piquancy of the dressing in this autumn salad which is particularly delicious with poultry.

1 lb (450 g) ripe eating plums
6 tblsp salad oil
2 tblsp wine vinegar
salt and pepper
pinch of sugar
1 tblsp fresh tarragon

1. Wash and wipe the plums. Split them in half and discard stones. Put into a serving dish.

2. Beat the oil and vinegar together and season with salt, pepper and sugar. Pour over the plums and chill.

3. Just before serving, stir the plums well and sprinkle with tarragon.

Cherry and Orange Salad

Morello cherries are dark, richly-flavoured and sharp, so that they need cooking before including in this unusual salad.

8 oz (225 g) Morello cherries
3 oranges
1 oz (25 g) sugar
¼ pint (150 ml) sweet white wine

1. Stone the cherries and place in a saucepan. Just cover with water and simmer until very tender but unbroken. Drain and place in a serving bowl.

2. Peel the oranges and remove all white pith. Cut the flesh across in thin slices and arrange on the cherries.

3. Sprinkle with sugar and pour on the wine. Cover and leave to stand for 1 hour before serving.

Cherry and Walnut Salad

The mixture of dark sweet cherries, crunchy walnuts and creamy dressing makes an irresistible summer salad, good with poultry, ham or fish.

8 oz (225 g) ripe black cherries
2 oz (50 g) walnut kernels
4 tblsp salad oil
2 tblsp wine vinegar
salt and pepper
2 tblsp double cream

1. Stone the cherries and place in a serving bowl.

2. Put the walnuts into another bowl and cover with boiling water. Leave to stand for 1 minute and then rub off the skins. Chop the walnuts roughly and add to the cherries.

3. Mix the oil and vinegar with salt and pepper. Pour over the cherries, stir well and leave to stand for 1 hour.

4. Just before serving, pour on the cream and serve at once.

Orange and Onion Salad

This is the perfect salad to serve with duck or game, but it is also excellent on its own as a very light meal.

4 oranges
1 medium onion
lettuce or chicory leaves
4 tblsp salad oil
2 tblsp wine vinegar
salt and pepper
1 tblsp chopped fresh mint

1. Peel the oranges and remove all white pith. Cut the flesh across in very thin slices, saving all the juice which runs out.

2. Peel the onion. Cut in very thin slices and push gently to separate into rings.

3. Arrange a bed of lettuce or chicory leaves on a serving plate. Arrange the orange slices in a layer on the leaves. Sprinkle with onion rings.

4. Mix the oil, vinegar, salt and pepper and pour over the salad. Sprinkle on the chopped mint.

Fruited Coleslaw

The contrasting textures and flavours of this salad make it an attractive side dish or a light meal.

1 lb (450 g) hard white cabbage
4 oz (100 g) white or black grapes
4 oz (100 g) slice of ripe melon
4 oz (100 g) black cherries
1 peach
1 eating apple
2 tblsp honey
½ pint (300 ml) soured cream
2 tsp lemon juice
salt and pepper
1 tblsp chopped fresh fennel or dill

1. Shred the cabbage finely and place in a bowl.

2. Prepare the fruit in a second bowl and do not mix until just before serving. Halve grapes and remove pips. Dice the melon and discard seeds and peel. Remove stones from cherries.

3. Peel the peach and dice the flesh. Do not peel the apple, but remove the core and dice the flesh. Sprinkle peach and apple with half the lemon juice.

4. Just before serving, mix the cabbage and all the fruit. Pour on the honey.

5. Season the soured cream with remaining lemon juice, salt and pepper. Pour into cabbage and fruit mixture and toss lightly.

6. Sprinkle with fennel or dill and serve.

Apple and Raisin Slaw

A variation on the traditional cabbage theme which is particularly good with rich meats like ham, pork or duck.

1 lb (450 g) hard white cabbage
4 oz (100 g) carrots
2 eating apples
1 tblsp lemon juice
2 oz (50 g) seedless raisins
½ pint (300 ml) mayonnaise
pinch of mustard powder

1. Shred the cabbage finely into a serving bowl. Grate the carrots and mix with the cabbage.

2. Do not peel the apples, but core and chop the flesh. Sprinkle with lemon juice.

3. Add the raisins, mayonnaise and mustard powder to the apples and mix well.

4. Add this mixture to the cabbage and mix well. Chill for 30 minutes before serving.

Apple and Bacon Salad

An unusual combination of ingredients which makes a refreshing first course to stimulate the appetite. If bacon is not liked, peeled prawns may be used instead.

8 oz (225 g) lean bacon
2 eating apples
1 tblsp lemon juice
3 celery sticks
1 oz (25 g) hazelnuts or walnut kernels
4 tblsp salad or nut oil
2 tblsp wine vinegar
salt and pepper
pinch of mustard powder
pinch of sugar
watercress or chicory

1. Grill the bacon until crisp. Crumble into small pieces.

2. Do not peel the apples, but core and chop the flesh. Sprinkle with lemon juice.

3. Chop the celery and nuts. Mix with apples and bacon.

4. Mix the oil, vinegar, salt, pepper, mustard and sugar.

5. Arrange a bed of watercress or chicory on a serving dish. Arrange the bacon mixture on top. Pour on the dressing and serve at once.

Strawberry Salad

A very good summer salad which goes well with poultry. The strawberries should be very large and ripe but firm.

1 lb (450 g) strawberries
4 tblsp mayonnaise
4 tblsp double cream
2 tsp caster sugar
lettuce leaves

1. Hull the strawberries. Reserve 6 berries and cut the rest in half lengthwise.

2. Mix the mayonnaise, cream and sugar together until evenly coloured.

3. Arrange a bed of lettuce on a serving dish. Arrange the halved berries on top in a mound.

4. Spoon the dressing over the berries. Garnish with the whole fruit.

Raspberry Salad

A refreshing salad to serve with poultry, ham or pork. It looks most attractive if arranged on individual side plates.

8 oz (225 g) raspberries
2 tblsp salad oil
1 tblsp lemon juice
salt and pepper
pinch of sugar
lettuce leaves

1. The berries should be ripe and very fresh. Place them in a bowl.

2. Mix the oil, lemon juice, salt, pepper and sugar. Pour over the fruit and leave to stand for 30 minutes.

3. Arrange a bed of lettuce leaves on a serving dish or individual plates. Spoon fruit and dressing into the centre and serve at once.

Cherry Cheese Salad

A light pretty salad which makes a simple luncheon dish, or a first course for a more formal meal.

1 lb (450 g) black cherries
4 oz (100 g) cream cheese
2 spring onions
4 tblsp salad oil
2 tblsp lemon juice
salt and pepper
4 oz (100 g) cucumber
lettuce leaves

1. Stone the cherries, saving any juice which runs out.

2. Put the cheese into a bowl. Chop the onions finely and mix into the cheese. Form into small balls the same size as the cherries.

3. Mix together the oil, lemon juice, salt and pepper, and any cherry juice.

4. Peel the cucumber and cut into dice.

5. Arrange a bed of lettuce in a serving bowl. Pile the cucumber on top. Mix the cherries and cheese balls together and place on top of the cucumber.

6. Pour on the dressing and serve at once.

Orange and Avocado Salad

This salad may be served in a bowl and is excellent with fish or poultry, or it may be served in the avocado skins.

2 thin-skinned oranges
2 avocado pears
3 tblsp oil
1 tblsp white wine vinegar
salt and pepper
1 tsp mint leaves

1. Grate the rind from 1 orange. Peel the orange and divide into segments, removing all pith and skin. Squeeze the juice from the second orange.

2. Cut the avocado pears in half and remove the stones. Scoop out the flesh and chop into small pieces. Mix with the orange segments and put into a serving bowl or return to the avocado skins.

3. Mix the orange rind, juice, oil, vinegar, salt, pepper and very finely chopped mint. Pour over the salad and serve at once.

Plum Salad

A delicious dish which can only be prepared when plums are very large, ripe and sweet, and which makes a complete meal.

12 large ripe plums
4 oz (100 g) cream cheese
1 small onion
1 tblsp capers
4 tblsp mayonnaise
2 tblsp double cream
lettuce leaves

1. Wash and dry the plums. Cut them in half and take out the stones.

2. Put the cheese into a bowl. Chop the onion very finely. Mix the onion and capers with the cheese, and fill the cavities of the plums.

3. Mix the mayonnaise and cream together until evenly coloured.

4. Arrange a bed of lettuce leaves on a serving dish. Place the plums cut-side down on the lettuce. Spoon over the dressing and serve at once.

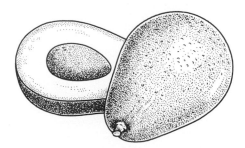

Celery, Orange and Onion Salad

A good winter salad with an interesting mixture of textures and flavours. It is particularly delicious served with rich meats such as pork or duck.

2 large oranges
1 medium onion
1 small head celery
6 tblsp olive oil
1 tblsp wine vinegar
salt and pepper

1. Peel the oranges very carefully to remove all trace of white pith. Cut the flesh across in thin slices, saving any juice which runs out.

2. Slice the onion very thinly and press out into rings.

3. Slice the celery very thinly.

4. Arrange the oranges, onion and celery in layers in a bowl.

5. Mix the reserved orange juice with oil, vinegar, salt and pepper and pour over the salad. Chill for 30 minutes before serving.

Grapefruit and Grape Salad

The mixture of slightly sharp grapefruit and sweet grapes makes an attractive first course or a salad to accompany poultry or fish.

2 grapefruit
4 oz (100 g) white grapes
4 tblsp oil
2 tblsp wine vinegar
1 tsp caster sugar
salt and pepper
2 tsp chopped fresh mint

1. Peel the grapefruit, removing all white pith. Using a very sharp knife, remove the segments without any skin. Place in a bowl with any juice which has run out.

2. Cut the grapes in half and remove pips. Mix grapes and grapefruit segments.

3. Mix the oil, vinegar, sugar, salt and pepper and pour over the fruit.

4. Mix well and sprinkle with mint. Chill for 30 minutes before serving.

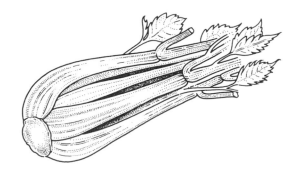

Winter Fruit Salad

Even when conventional salad vegetables are in short supply, it is possible to prepare a tasty and nourishing salad from store-cupboard ingredients.

1 banana
1 eating apple
1 tblsp lemon juice
3 oz (75 g) dates or figs
2 oz (50 g) nut kernels
2 oz (50 g) grated Cheddar cheese
4 tblsp oil
1 tblsp wine vinegar
salt and pepper

1. Peel the banana and cut into thick slices. Do not peel the apple, but remove core and cut flesh into thin slices. Mix banana and apple in a bowl and sprinkle with lemon juice.

2. Chop the dates or figs and the nuts. Mix with the other fruit.

3. Sprinkle on the grated cheese.

4. Mix the oil, vinegar, salt and pepper and pour over the salad. Toss well and serve at once.

Pineapple Coleslaw

Fruit-flavoured coleslaw is particularly delicious with frankfurters or other delicatessen meats.

12 oz (350 g) hard white cabbage
8 oz (225 g) can pineapple cubes
3 celery sticks
2 tblsp chopped mixed nuts
3 tblsp mayonnaise
3 tblsp sour cream
salt and pepper
pinch of sugar

1. Shred the cabbage finely and place in a bowl.

2. Drain the pineapple cubes and add to the cabbage.

3. Chop the celery finely and add to the salad with the nuts.

4. Beat the mayonnaise with the sour cream, salt, pepper and sugar. Pour over the salad and toss well.

JELLIED SALADS

Tomato Jelly Ring with Salad Filling

Fresh-tasting tomato jelly is a foil for a delicious accompaniment of freshly cooked summer vegetables.

¾ pint (450 ml) tomato juice
strip of lemon rind
1 tsp concentrated tomato purée
4 peppercorns
1 bay leaf
salt and pepper
pinch of sugar
1 garlic clove, crushed
½ oz (15 g) gelatine
3 tblsp cold water
1 tblsp lemon juice

4 hardboiled eggs
¼ pint (150 ml) mayonnaise
8 oz (225 g) shelled peas
8 oz (225 g) young carrots
8 oz (225 g) shelled broad beans
8 oz (225 g) French beans
8 oz (225 g) small new potatoes
6 tblsp salad oil
3 tblsp wine vinegar
salt and pepper
pinch of sugar
pinch of mustard powder

1. Put the tomato juice into a pan with lemon rind, purée, peppercorns, bay leaf, salt, pepper, sugar and garlic. Bring slowly to the boil, and simmer for 5 minutes.

2. Stir the gelatine into the cold water and put into a pan of hot water until the gelatine is syrupy. Add the lemon juice.

3. Strain the hot tomato mixture. Stir in the gelatine. Pour into a wetted ring mould and leave to set.

4. Chop the eggs roughly and mix with mayonnaise.

5. Cook peas, carrots, broad beans, French beans and potatoes in separate pans. Drain well and cool.

6. Mix together the oil, vinegar, salt, pepper, sugar and mustard. Sprinkle some of the dressing over each type of cooked vegetable.

7. Turn the tomato jelly ring on to a serving plate. Fill the centre with egg mayonnaise. Arrange heaps of cooked vegetables round the tomato ring, and sprinkle with any remaining dressing.

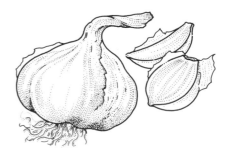

Jellied Beetroot Salad

When beetroot is prepared in this way, it does not 'leak' over salad ingredients. The flavour of the jelly enhances the flavour of the vegetable.

1 lb (450 g) beetroot
1 packet raspberry jelly
¾ pint (450 ml) boiling water
2 tblsp wine vinegar

1. Boil the beetroot until the skins slip off easily. Cool and cut into neat dice.

2. Make up the jelly with the boiling water and stir in the vinegar. Leave until the jelly is cool and syrupy.

3. Stir in the beetroot and pour into a serving dish. Chill until firm.

4. Do not turn out the jellied beetroot, but serve with a spoon.

Jellied Cucumber Salad
Serves 6

If this is made in a ring mould, the centre may be filled with seafood or chicken.

1 packet lime jelly
½ pint (300 ml) boiling water
4 tblsp lemon juice
1 small onion
¼ pint (150 ml) mayonnaise
¼ pint (150 ml) soured cream
1 small cucumber

1. Make up the jelly with the boiling water. Add the lemon juice and grated onion. Leave until cool and syrupy.

2. Stir in the mayonnaise and soured cream.

3. Do not peel the cucumber. Grate the cucumber and stir into the jelly mixture.

4. Place in 6 individual moulds or 1 large one. Chill until set and unmould on to a serving dish. Garnish if liked with watercress or with thinly sliced cucumber.

Tomato Lemon Jelly Salad

A quickly made tomato jelly which provides a smooth and savoury contrast to a crunchy fresh salad.

1 packet lemon jelly
¼ pint (150 ml) boiling water
½ pint (300 ml) tomato juice
1 tblsp wine vinegar
2 tsp Worcestershire sauce
salt and pepper
4 tomatoes
1 small cucumber
4 celery sticks
1 eating apple
4 tblsp mayonnaise

1. Put the jelly and boiling water into a small thick saucepan and heat gently until dissolved. Remove from heat and stir in tomato juice.

2. Add vinegar, sauce, salt and pepper. Mix well and pour into a ring mould. Chill until firm.

3. Skin the tomatoes and remove pips. Chop the flesh finely.

4. Peel the cucumber and dice the flesh. Chop the celery finely.

5. Do not peel the apples, but core them and dice finely.

6. Mix the tomatoes, cucumber, celery and apple with the mayonnaise.

7. Unmould the tomato ring on to a serving plate. Fill the centre with the salad. Serve immediately.

Apple Salad Ring

This winter salad relieves heavy meals and helps to sharpen the appetite. A little more sugar may be added if the apples are very sharp, but the jellied ring should not be sweet.

1½ lb (675 g) cooking apples
3 oz (75 g) sugar
juice of 1 lemon
1 tblsp gelatine
3 tblsp water
4 celery sticks
1 eating apple
3 oz (75 g) walnut kernels

1. Peel and core the apples. Slice them and put into a pan with the sugar and ½ pint (300 ml) water. Simmer until the apples have collapsed completely.

2. Reserve 1 tablespoon lemon juice. Add the rest to the apples and simmer until the mixture is smooth and thick.

3. Dissolve the gelatine in water in a bowl over hot water, until the gelatine is syrupy. Stir into the apple purée, and pour into a mould. Chill until firm.

4. Just before serving, prepare the salad. Chop the celery and the apple without peeling. Mix with the nuts. Sprinkle with lemon juice.

5. Unmould the apple jelly and fill or surround with the salad.

Jellied Cheese Salad

A sharply flavoured cheese mould which is the perfect partner to a mixed salad.

8 oz (225 g) cottage cheese
1 oz (25 g) blue cheese
1 tblsp gelatine
¼ pint (150 ml) evaporated milk
pinch of mustard powder
salt and pepper
lettuce leaves
cucumber, tomatoes, radishes, cooked vegetables

1. Sieve the cottage cheese and blue cheese together.

2. Put the gelatine into a small bowl with 2 tablespoons water. Stand the bowl in a pan of hot water and stir over low heat until the gelatine is syrupy. Leave until cool.

3. Stir the gelatine into the evaporated milk and then beat into the cheese mixture until well blended.

4. Season well to taste with mustard, salt and pepper and beat again.

5. Pour into a small oiled mould or into four individual dishes. Chill.

6. Arrange a bed of lettuce leaves on a serving dish. Unmould the cheese on to the lettuce.

7. Chop cucumber, skinned tomatoes, radishes or any cooked vegetables available. Mix together and arrange round the cheese moulds.

SALAD DRESSINGS

French Dressing

Chopped mixed fresh herbs may be added to this dressing, and some people like to add a pinch of sugar.

6 tblsp olive or salad oil
2 tblsp wine vinegar or lemon juice
pinch of mustard powder
salt and pepper

1. Put the ingredients into a screwtop jar and shake vigorously, or beat together in a bowl.

2. The oil will float to the top if the dressing is left to stand, and it will need shaking or beating again before use.

Mayonnaise

The oil should be at room temperature when making mayonnaise, and it is best to use a warm bowl. Mix with a wooden spoon or whisk, and add the oil very slowly. If the mixture curdles, put another egg yolk into a bowl, and whisk in the curdled mixture very slowly.

2 egg yolks
pinch of mustard powder
salt and pepper
½ pint (300 ml) olive or salad oil
2 tblsp wine vinegar or lemon juice

1. Mix the egg yolks, mustard, salt and pepper in a bowl until well blended.

2. Add the oil drop by drop, whisking or beating with a wooden spoon. As the sauce thickens, add the oil a little more quickly.

3. When the oil has been used, add vinegar or lemon juice to get the required consistency.

4. If necessary, store in a screwtop jar in a cool place, but not a refrigerator.

Easy Mayonnaise

The use of a whole egg makes this a very easy mayonnaise to prepare. It may be made with a balloon whisk, or with an electric blender.

1 large egg
1 tblsp lemon juice or wine vinegar
1 tsp sugar
½ tsp salt
¼ tsp white pepper
¼ tsp mustard powder
½ pint (300 ml) olive or salad oil

1. Put the egg into a bowl with the lemon juice or vinegar, sugar, salt, pepper and mustard. Stir into a paste.

2. Add the oil, drop by drop, beating until the mixture is thick and creamy.

3. Keep cool, but do not chill.

Cooked Salad Cream

Many people prefer this to mayonnaise as it is not so rich. If stored in a cool place, the salad cream will keep up to six weeks.

4 oz (100 g) block margarine
3 oz (75 g) plain flour
3 oz (75 g) sugar
½ oz (15 g) mustard powder
1½ pints (900 ml) milk
2 eggs
¾ pint (450 ml) vinegar
salt and pepper

1. Melt the margarine over low heat.

2. Remove from heat and stir in flour, sugar, mustard and a little milk to make a smooth paste.

3. Return to the heat and cook gently, stirring all the time, and gradually adding the remaining milk. Cook until the mixture is thick and smooth.

4. Remove from heat and beat well. Leave until cool and beat in the eggs.

5. Beat in the vinegar slowly, a little at a time, until the mixture is smooth and creamy. Season to taste with salt and pepper.

6. Put into sterilized screwtop jars and store in a cool place.

Coleslaw Dressing

The correct dressing for cabbage salads is thick and creamy with a noticeable mustard flavour.

2 tsp sugar
2 tsp plain flour
2 tsp mustard powder
1 tsp salt
pinch of cayenne pepper
5 tblsp wine vinegar
1 egg yolk
8 tblsp double cream
1 tsp softened butter

1. Mix sugar, flour, mustard, salt, pepper and vinegar in a bowl. Place over a pan of boiling water and heat, stirring until the mixture thickens.

2. Cool to lukewarm. Add egg yolk, cream and butter and beat well.

Danish Blue Cheese Dressing

Dressing made with blue cheese has a welcome tang which goes well with green salads.

¼ pint (150 ml) olive oil
¼ pint (150 ml) lemon juice
1 tblsp sugar
1 tsp salt
1 tsp paprika
2 oz (50 g) Danish Blue cheese

1. Put the oil, lemon juice, sugar, salt and paprika into a screwtop jar and shake well.

2. Grate the cheese finely. Add to the jar and shake very well. Chill before serving.

Horseradish Cream Dressing

This distinctive dressing is particularly good for beetroot, tomato or potato salad. Add the horseradish with discretion as it can be very strong if freshly grated (the bottled variety may be used).

1 tsp made mustard
1 tsp sugar
½ tsp salt
¼ tsp pepper
¼ pint (150 ml) evaporated milk
¼ pint (150 ml) olive oil
3 tblsp wine vinegar
1-2 tblsp grated horseradish
squeeze of lemon juice

1. Mix the mustard, sugar, salt and pepper together and stir in the evaporated milk.

2. Whisk in the olive oil, little by little. Gradually add the vinegar which will thicken the dressing.

3. Stir in the horseradish and lemon juice. Adjust seasoning to taste.

Fruit Salad Dressing

This refreshing dressing is particularly good with any raw fruit being used as a salad with savoury foods, but it is also a slimming dressing with other types of salad.

¼ pint (150 ml) natural yoghurt
3 tblsp orange juice
1 tblsp lemon juice
1 tblsp rose hip syrup

1. Put the yoghurt, orange juice, lemon juice and syrup into a bowl.

2. Beat with a fork until smooth.

3. Chill before serving over fruit or other salad.

Sour Cream Dressing

This is a good substitute for mayonnaise, and is particularly pleasant for a potato salad, perhaps with the addition of chopped celery and apple.

¼ pint (150 ml) soured cream
2 tsp rose hip syrup
¼ tsp salt
¼ tsp onion or garlic salt
½ tsp Worcestershire sauce
2 tsp vinegar

1. Put all ingredients into a bowl and beat together with a fork until well blended.

2. Chill for 30 minutes before using.

Mustard Dressing

A light and tasty dressing which is good with potato salad, or with coleslaw made from red or white cabbage.

¼ pint (150 ml) soured cream
1 tsp made mustard
1 tsp caster sugar
½ tsp finely grated onion
¼ tsp salt
1 tblsp chopped fresh parsley

Dressing Without Oil or Egg

A pleasant salad dressing for those who cannot include oil or egg in their diets. It will keep for a month in a cool place.

1 tblsp sugar
1 tsp salt
¼ tsp white pepper
2 tsp made mustard
¼ pint (150 ml) evaporated milk
6 tblsp wine vinegar

1. Mix the sugar, salt, pepper and mustard in the bottom of a small bowl.

2. Gradually work in the evaporated milk until well blended.

3. Add the vinegar drop by drop to prevent curdling, mixing gently until well blended.

4. Put into small dry jars with vinegar-proof lids. Store in a cool place.

1. Put the soured cream into a bowl and work in the remaining ingredients.

2. Chill for 30 minutes before using.

Apple Yoghurt Dressing

This is a good slimmer's dressing if made with low-fat yoghurt. It may be served with fruit or vegetable salads.

¼ pint (150 ml) natural yoghurt
3 tblsp apple juice
pinch of ground cinnamon
pinch of ground ginger
pinch of salt

1. Put the yoghurt into a bowl. Whisk in the apple juice with a fork.

2. Season to taste with cinnamon, ginger and salt. Chill for 20 minutes before serving.

Garlic Sauce

This strongly-flavoured sauce may be used with lightly cooked vegetables or with raw vegetables and is an alternative to plain mayonnaise for those who enjoy garlic.

3 large garlic cloves
2 egg yolks
salt and pepper
1 tsp mustard powder
7 fl oz (175 ml) olive oil
1 tsp lemon juice

1. Crush the garlic cloves. Work into the egg yolks with salt, pepper and mustard, and mix well.

2. Add the oil gradually, drop by drop, beating with a wooden spoon or wire whisk.

3. When all the oil has been incorporated and the mixture is thick, stir in the lemon juice.

Slimmer's Juice Dressing

A light dressing for green salads which may be varied by the substitution of a mixture of orange and lemon juice instead of the tomato flavour.

1 thin slice of onion
1 tblsp chopped fresh parsley or mint
4 tblsp tomato juice
1 tsp made mustard
salt and pepper

1. Chop the onion very finely and mix with parsley or mint.

2. Add the tomato juice, mustard, salt and pepper and mix very well. Chill before serving.

*For a smoother dressing, place all ingredients in a liquidizer and blend until the onion and herbs are very finely chopped.

Yoghurt Dressing

Good on all types of salads, this goes particularly well with beetroot, tomatoes and cucumbers. Low-fat yoghurt may be used for dietary purposes.

¼ pint (150 ml) natural yoghurt
juice of ½ lemon
salt and pepper
1 tblsp chopped fresh parsley

1. Mix together the yoghurt and lemon juice.

2. Season well with salt and pepper. Stir in parsley.

3. Serve separately, or pour over salad just before serving.

Lemon Dressing

This is a good dressing for those who dislike vinegar and which is suitable for all types of salads.

1 small onion
1 oz (25 g) pickled gherkin
1 hardboiled egg
1 tsp capers
1 tsp chopped fresh mint, parsley or tarragon
5 tblsp oil
3 tblsp lemon juice
salt and pepper

1. Chop the onion, gherkin, egg and capers very finely with the herbs (this may be done in a liquidizer if liked but the mixture should not be a purée).

2. Mix in the oil and lemon juice and season well with salt and pepper.

3. Chill for 15 minutes before serving so that the flavours blend.

Sweet Yoghurt Dressing

A dressing which should be chilled before serving on salads which contain fruit or dried fruit. Low-fat yoghurt may be used.

½ pint (300 ml) natural yoghurt
2 tblsp clear honey
1 tblsp orange juice
1 tblsp lemon juice
1 tsp grated lemon rind

1. Beat the yoghurt very lightly in a bowl.

2. Stir together the honey, orange juice, lemon juice and rind until completely mixed.

3. Gradually add honey mixture to yoghurt, beating lightly.

4. Chill before serving.

INDEX